Management of Soil Structure

NIPA® GENX ELECTRONIC RESOURCES & SOLUTIONS P. LTD.
New Delhi-110 034

About the Author

Dr. Anandkumar Naorem, currently employed as a scientist at ICAR-Central Arid Zone Research Institute in Jodhpur, India, previously held the position of Head-in-charge at ICAR-CAZRI, RRS-Bhuj, India. He completed his bachelor's degree at Assam Agricultural University, Assam, India, and pursued his master's degree in soil microbiology and bioformulation at the College of Post-Graduate Studies, Central Agricultural University, Meghalaya, India. His doctoral research, conducted at Bidhan Chandra Krishi Viswavidyalaya in West Bengal, India, focused on the remediation of soil heavy metals for safer crop cultivation.

Dr. Naorem, who has authored several national and international publications, has received national recognition, including the 2015 Best Zonal Master's Thesis award from the Indian Society of Soil Science and the UGC-Maulana Azad National Fellowship for Minority Students (India). He is acknowledged for his contributions as a young scientist by numerous societies and organizations, having led various research projects on soil quality in arid regions, studies on elevated carbon dioxide levels, and investigations into halophytes. Notably, he has played a key role in international initiatives promoting spineless cactus as a dryland feed option in Gujarat.

---

for other volumes of
The Professional's Notes Series

The Professional's Notes Series

Volume 02

Management of Soil Structure

Anandkumar Naorem
Scientist, Division of IFS
ICAR-Central Arid Zone Research Institute
Ministry of A&Fw, Government of India
Jodhpur-342003, Rajasthan, India

NIPA® GENX ELECTRONIC RESOURCES & SOLUTIONS P. LTD.
New Delhi-110 034

NIPA® GENX ELECTRONIC RESOURCES & SOLUTIONS P. LTD.

101,103, Vikas Surya Plaza, CU Block
L.S.C.Market, Pitam Pura, New Delhi-110 034
Ph : +91 11 27341616, 27341717, 27341718
E-mail: newindiapublishingagency@gmail.com
www: www.nipabooks.com

For customer assistance, please contact
Phone: + 91-11-27 34 17 17
Fax: + 91-11- 27 34 16 16
E-Mail: feedbacks@nipabooks.com

Print ISBN: 978-93-58875-75-1

ebook ISBN: 978-93-58873-21-4

Composed and Designed by NIPA®.

Preface

Welcome to Volume 02, dedicated to the "Management of Soil Structure." Within these pages, we will be dealing with the intricate world of soil management practices aimed at preserving and enhancing the physical properties of soil. To truly understand soil and its ecological dynamics, we must first grasp the significance of its physical properties. Soil physical properties serve as crucial indicators of soil quality, providing insights into its structure, texture, porosity, and water-holding capacity. These properties not only influence the physical characteristics of soil but also play a pivotal role in regulating nutrient dynamics, biological health, and soil fertility. A fundamental understanding of soil physical properties is essential for unravelling the complex interplay between soil structure, nutrient availability, and biological activity. Soil structure, for example, affects nutrient exchange and microbial colonization, thus influencing soil fertility and biological health. Similarly, soil porosity affects water infiltration and drainage, which in turn impact nutrient leaching, root growth, and microbial activity.

Research on soil physical properties is built upon these foundational concepts, aiming to elucidate the mechanisms governing soil structure, nutrient dynamics, and ecosystem function. By examining the relationships between soil texture, porosity, compaction, and other physical attributes, researchers can develop predictive models and management strategies to optimize soil health and productivity. Moreover, understanding soil physical properties is essential for designing sustainable land management practices that promote soil conservation, water retention, and nutrient cycling. By integrating knowledge of soil physics with principles of ecology, agronomy, and hydrology, researchers and practitioners can develop holistic approaches to soil management that enhance soil fertility, resilience, and ecosystem sustainability.

As we discuss into the depths of soil structure management in this volume, let us remember the importance of soil physical properties as key determinants of soil quality and ecosystem health. May the insights and knowledge shared within these pages empower readers to become stewards of soil structure, fostering healthy soils, resilient ecosystems, and a sustainable future for generations to come.

With gratitude and anticipation

Anandkumar Naorem

Contents

Management of soil structure

For single grain structured soil

- placement of impermeable asphalt barriers in deep sands at depths of 55-60 cm.
- Application of organic manures or pond sediments.

For moderately coarse or coarse

- addition of organic manure.
- pond sediments or clayey soil.

For fine textured soils

- Tillage at optimum moisture level. - friable consistency.

For acid/alkaline soils

- liming materials.
- gypsum
- green manuring/organic manures.

Soil aggregation

→ Clay - Polyvalent cation - clay
→ clay - OM - clay
→ clay - Polyvalent cation - OM - clay
→ clay - Polyvalent cation - OM - silt plus sand.

Types of soil crust

i) Structural crusts

a) slaking crusts: formed due to disintegration of a sodic or weakly aggregated soil by impact of raindrops.
: thin dense layer - sharp boundary with underlying layer, no observable textural separation

b) Infiltrating crusts: formed on medium textured - due to impact of rain drops - separation of silt particles and sealing of void space.
- clear textural sep.

c) Coalescing crusts : formed in wet soils when the soil material is in viscous state by the drop energy driving force.
- generally thick (upto 20 mm) – more densely packed than underlying horizon. – ~~som~~ exhibit gradual transitions with underlying layer – so called transitional microhorizons

d) Sieving crusts : formed by the impact of raindrops on sandy soils – leading to sorting of soil particles causing concn of coarser part at top and finer in deeper position,

so two contrasting layers
- uppermost 1-5 mm (consists of loosely packed coarser ~~skeleton~~ grains)
- lower – 100 μm – 1 mm (fine particles)

ii) Erosion and depositional crusts

a) Erosional crusts : formed from the erosion of sieving crusts when loosely coarse textured upper layer – stripped away by overland flow – leaving only layer of fine particles.

b) Depositional crusts : formed after sealing of the surface by a structural crust and concn of detached particle from eroded clods in interclods ~~depos~~ microdeposition or furrows through micro scale runoff.

c) Cryptogamic crusts : surface crusts made of algae, fungi, lichens, mosses, bac. – also known as microphytic crusts.
↳ sometimes not considered as soil crust.

Organic Matter
(Soil aggregation)

- cationic bridge
- hydrogen bonding
- Vander waal's force
- sesquioxide humus complex

pF values of soil consistency

- Atterberg (1912) (Swedish agriculturist) – four forms of soil consistency excluding viscous state.

a) Hard/harsh consistency : pF > 4.5 (>31 Bar)
b) Friable or soft : pF 4.5–2.8 (31–0.62)
c) Plastic consistency : pF 2.8–0.5 (0.62–0.003)
d) Sticky " : pF 0.5–0 (0.003–0.001)
e) Viscous : for saturated soil pF 0 (0.001). – soil flows either under pressure or merely by gravity.

Factors affecting soil consist

- Soil water content — due to two main forces < molecular attract, surface tension.
  — large in dry range (due to cohesion)
  — " " wet " (due to adhesion)
  — small in moist range and saturated
- Texture : — sufficient clay – exhibit consistency.
  — consis. ↑ with ↑ in clay content
- Type of clay — expanding – more consis. because of ↑ surface charge and more specific surface
- Organic matter – more consistency than sand & silt but < than clay.
- Structure : well aggregated soils ↓ consistency than puddled.
  ∴ Alkali soil more consistency than non alkali floculated soil.

Atterberg's Limits

- 4 limits < floculation limit, upper plastic limit, lower " ", shrinkage limit
- 2 constants < Plasticity Index, shrinkage ratio.

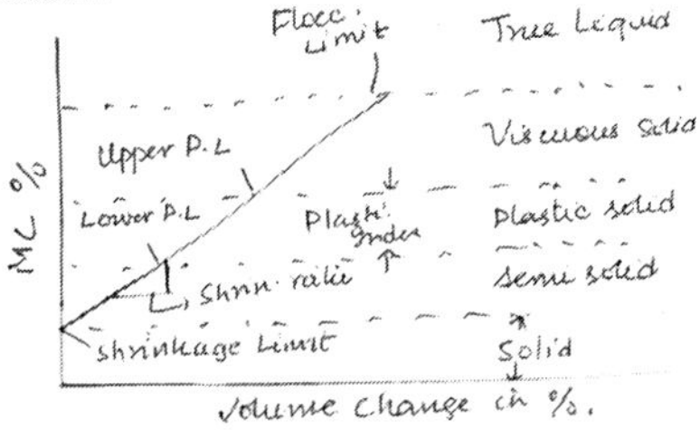

- Flocculation limit : when a mixture of soil and H_2O is in highly dispersed condition – represent true liquid. If m/c ↓ by evaporation – soil changed from true liquid to viscous liquid — min^m m/c at which this change - flocc. limit

Upper Plastic limit (pF 0.5) – 3.2 cm of H_2O

Lower " " (pF ~~2.8~~) – ~~3.3 cm of H_2O~~ 666/2 . 666 – 2000 cm of H_2O
↳ 2.8 – 3.3

Shrinkage Limit

- wc below which soil ceases to shrink – shrinkage limit.
- further ↓ wc of the soil no effect on change in volume.
- m/c at which soil changes from semisolid to solid.

Plasticity Index or Plastic no

– function of films and represents amt of H_2O that must be added to the soil system to increase the value of distance from a film thickness at which maxm tension occurs to a thickness at which flow is produced.

Shrinkage ratio

= change in volume per unit change in soil H_2O content

= slope of the line between plastic limit and shrink. limit.

$$= \frac{\text{given vol. change exp. as \% of dry volume}}{\text{change in } H_2O \text{ content above shrinkage limit.}}$$

$$= \frac{\frac{V_1 - V_2}{V_d} \times 100}{w_1 - w_2}$$

$$= \frac{\gamma_d}{\gamma_w} \text{ – dry density}$$

Volumetric shrinkage

$$VS = \frac{V_1 - V_d}{V_d} \times 100.$$

$$VS = (W_1 - W_S)\, SR$$

↳ mass H_2O content at shrinkage limit

Linear Shrinkage

$$L_S = 100\left[1 - \left[\frac{100}{VS + 100}\right]^{1/3}\right]$$

Significance of Atterberg limits and constants

- Index for physical classification of soil.
- ↳ ↑ upper plastic limit — large quantity of clay part (fine); abundance of plate like particles.
  ↳ ↑ Plastic no: — abundance of plate like particles
  — highly plastic.

- Index of accm of clay within the soil profile
- Index of soil tilth (best index)
- Shrinkage limit: optimum conditions for tillage because at this condition, the individual part granules are soft — cohesion is at minimum.
- significance of each limits

Consistency	Plasticity
- resistance to deform at moisture content of the soil in the field and are a manifestation of various forces of cohesion and adhesion within soil at various moist. contents	- soil
- usually evaluated on undisturbed soil aggregates	- disturbed, often wetted or moulded soil material. ↳ inherent soil property

- Law of plastic and viscous flow:

Plastic: Bingham equation

$V = K\mu (F - f)$

V — volume of flow; K — constant; μ — coeff. of mobility; F — force applied; f — force necessary to overcome cohesive force of the system

Viscous: Bingham's eqn → if f = 0.

$V = K\mu F$.

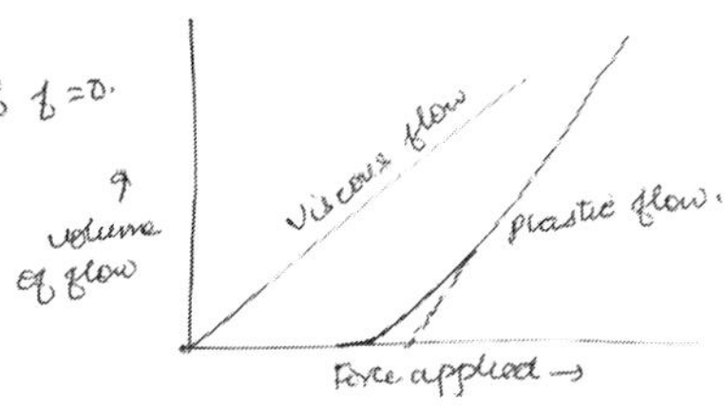

Factors affecting plastic limits and plasticity number

@
→ Clay content

- >15% clay
- ↑clay >15% → water contents of both limits ↑ → lower slightly but upper rapidly — ↑ in Plasticity no (index)
- plasticity Index – function of clay content – as it represents amt of water in a given no. of films from the lower plastic limit to upper plastic limit.

(b)
→ Nature of clay minerals

- Tectosilicates – non plastic
- Phylosilicates like kaolinite, montm etc – plastic
- PI ↑ with ↑ in specific surface.
- PI ↑ much more in montmor. – due to ↑ hydration
- PI ↓ in salt solution because of prevention of interlayer swelling and reduction of the thickness of diffuse double layer.

(c)
→ Nature of exchang. cations

- Expanding clays: – monovalent Na^+ & K^+ ↓ Plastic limits.
- K → ↓ lower plastic limit slightly } → ↓ PI.
  → ↓ lower upper limit rapidly
- Na^+ – lower plastic limit rapidly ↓ } ↑ PI.
  – upper " " slightly ↓
- Divalent cations – Ca^{2+} and Mg^{2+} – ↓ both plastic limits → but increases PI as because lower plastic limits rapidly ↓, and upper ↓ slightly.
- Exc. H^+ → ↑ PI both plastic limits ↓.

→ variations due to diffe. in hydration of clays saturated with diff. cations.

- Lower Plastic limit – lowest in Na sat. soil f.b K^+ sat.
  ↳ highest in Ca/Mg sat soil with expan. clay.

- upper plastic limit — lowest K^+-sat f.b Na^+ sat
  — highest Ca/Mg sat. soil.

- Plasticity number/Index containing expan. clays — highest Na-sat f.b K^+-sat.
- Mg saturated soil ↑ PI than Ca-sat soil.
  → due to variation in hydration of clays saturated with diff cations

- In non-expanding/partially expanding clays
  - exc. Na^+ ↓ lower plastic limit
  - exc K^+ ↓ lower and upper PL and PI as comp. with exc Ca/Mg
  - PI lowest — K sat f.b H/sat and highest in Mg sat.
  - PI ↑ in Ca^{2+} sat than Na^+-sat

(d) Organic matter content

→ ↑ OM → ↑ plastic limits but PN unchanged — due to effect of hydration.

- OM – high capacity for absorption of water — hydration of OM completed before formation of water film around the mineral particles.
  → so, water content at both plastic limits ↑ with ↑ in OM.

Measurement of Plastic Limits

- Casagrande Liquid Limit device
- ~~cutting~~ edge of grooving tool.

Soil swell-shrink potential	COLE
Low	<0.03
Moderate	0.03-0.06
High	0.06-0.09
very High	>0.09

Measurement of Shrinkage

$$COLE = \frac{Lm - 1}{Ld}$$

(Lm — length of moist soil; Ld — dry)

$$COLE = \frac{Lm}{Ld} - 1$$

$$COLE = \sqrt[3]{\frac{\rho_{bd}}{\rho_{bm}}} - 1$$

(ρ_{bd} — bulk density of dry (oven dry); ρ_{bm} — moist.)

If COLE > 0.09 — significant shrink and swelling.
>0.03 — presence of sign. amount of montmori or other swelling

Compaction

↳ soil particles are artificially rearranged and packed together into a closer state by mechanical means ie applied pressure or loads. — reducing total soil porosity, decreasing volume and increasing bulk density of the soil.

Consolidation

↳ gradual process of volume reduction of either initially saturated soil or compacted to the point of saturation of soilmass by expulsion of water from void space by applied pressure or loads.

Compression

— reduction in volume of dry/wet/satur. soil by appl^n of an external load or force on the soil.

Factors affecting soil compaction

a) Soil water content

- Dry soil – difficult to compact to high ρ_b due to incompressible nature of soil particles and high internal friction.
- As soil wc ↑ – thickness of water films around the particles ↑, ↓ cohesion — allowing to slide over each other.
- compactness ↑ – till a max^m value of mc. — optimum H_2O content for max^m compaction –↑ behaves like a fluid – loses its load bearing properties

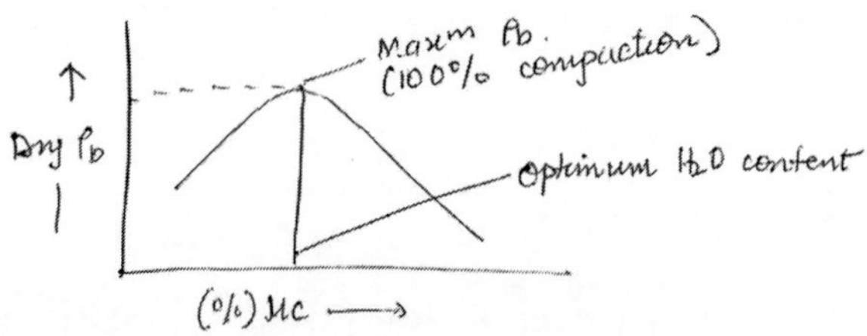

b) Applied pressure or load (Compactive effort)

- compactness ↑ ~~with~~ at a given MC → ↑ exponentially with ↑ in app. pressure. – then decreases at optimum MC.

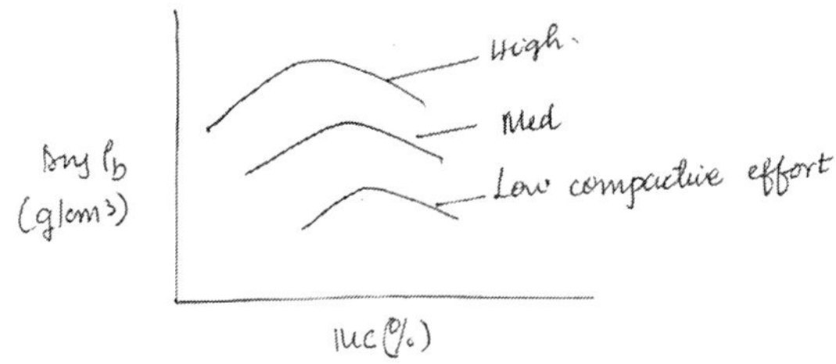

c) Soil Texture

ρb of coarse textured ↑ than ρb of fine textured because total pore spaces in clay higher – so normal compactness becomes maxm in coarse textured and decreases it goes finer.

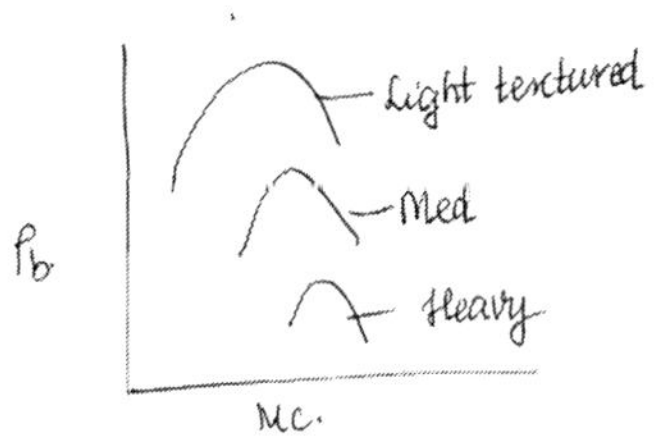

d) Amount of manipulation

↳ Continued compaction → remove total air ~~sp~~ filled pores.

if continued – complete reduction of pore spaces.

- Plant root growth – severely affected by compaction causing < 10% aeration porosity.
- Penetration resistance value 2 - 2.5MPa – critical limit for plant root elongation

---

- Tests compaction by Abbot's compaction apparatus.

Soil compaction	Soil consolidation
– densification of an unsat. soil mass by applied pressure	– dens. of sat. soil.
– almost an instantaneous phenomenon	– time dependent
– process of reducing pore space by expulsion of air through applied pressure or load	– ↓ pore volume – ~~changes mass wetness~~. by expulsion of water.
– causes ↓ air filled pore space without change in mass wetness	– ↓ pore volume by squeezing out H_2O – changes mass wetness.
– great agricultural signif. as it is related to pore charac.	– for engineers for foundation of building.

Soil compaction	Soil crusting
– defn	– defn.
– may develop anywhere in soil profile – thickness more than a crust layer	– formed over exposed soils in upper few mm.
– not essential.	– dispersion of fine soil part followed by rapid drying – essential
– low OM, high sand and low clay.	– low om, high silt and high exc. Na^+ % ESP
– all textural types.	– formed in all soil textural types except sand. ↑ with ↑ silt content

Soil water (compilation)

- Vander Waals radius of H → 1.2 A°
- O → 1.4 A°
- covalent bond distance H – O → 0.97 A° O. quote
  H – H → 1.54 A° laser.
- H+ atoms attached with O at any angle of 103°–106° (avg 105°) 104.59
- –ve charge on O → due to unshared lone pair of e⁻
- +ve " " H → due to unscreened +ve charge of protons of H atoms.

↓

arrangement — dipoles — H bonding with neighbouring mol.

- space occupied by H_2O mol – depends on O⁻ ion – 2.64 A°.
- 1 cm3 of water molecule (liquid) contains 3.346×10^{22} mol.

  $\left(\frac{6.023}{18} \times 10^{23} = 3.346 \times 10^{22}\right)$

- H_2O-polymer of H-bonded molecules.
- Ice – complete hydrogen bonding
  - one H_2O mol. bonded with 4 neighbouring mol → open hexagonal layer lattice
  → when melted – rigid structure partially broken down – additional H_2O mol. enters in the intermolecular space – each H_2O mol surrounded by more than 4 neig. H_2O mol.
  → so denser
- Liquid water – absorbs 80 cal/gm (solid – liquid)
- Flickering cluster model
  - H-bonded H_2O molecules microcrystals embedded in a matrix of non hydrogen bonded molecules.
- H-bond – so strong – ↑ B.P, M.P, dielectric constant, surface tension etc
- Density
  - low density due to open structure
  - maxm density at 4 °C (1 Mg/m3)

50°C (0.988)
↑ – due to more kinetic motion – more space
4 °C
↓
0°C (0.99 Mg/m3)
↳ due to hexagonal arr.
↳ more space.

- density of ice: 0.917 Mg/m³
- density of soil water: 0.97 – 0.98 Mg/m³ (act like ice)
- Ice like structure extends upto 60 Å from the soil surface.
- surface tension
- tension of the surface water film caused by attractn of the particles in surface layer by bulk of liquid thus ↓ surface area.
- ergs/cm² or dynes/cm
- [MT-2]
- Temperature ↑ and addition of electrolytes ↑ → S.T. ↑ due to more affinity of solute mol. than H_2O mol to each other.

due to ↓ density → ↓ cohesive force at surface as well as liquid

↓

so S.T. ↓ linearly

- contact angle — angle between the interface of gas, liquid and solid and represented by S.T

$$\cos\theta = \frac{\gamma_{GS} - \gamma_{LS}}{\gamma_{GL}}$$

← It determines the wettability of a solid surface using young equation
- measured using goniometer

If θ = 0 = complete/perfect wetting ←

θ = <90° = wetting the solid ←

90 - 180° = not to wet the solid ←

= 180° → complete non-wetting ←

0 - complete wetting
<90 - hydrophilic
>90 - hydrophobic

- Capillarity — ability of a fluid to flow in narrow spaces.

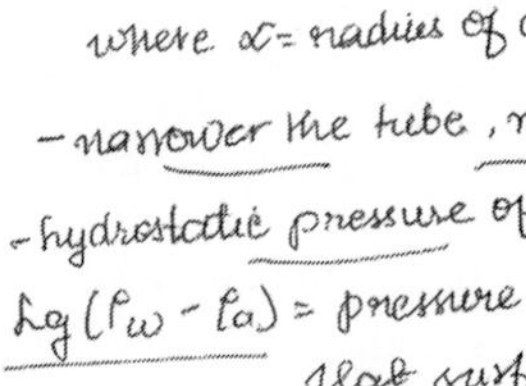

- Pressure diff. on two sides of menisci – depends on radius of curvature.
- Pressure below the menisci < atm pressure less by $2\gamma/\alpha$

where α = radius of curvature.

- narrower the tube, more smaller α → larger press. diff.
- hydrostatic pressure of 'h' cm column of water

$hg(\rho_w - \rho_a)$ = pressure diff. between curved menisci and flat surface

$= \frac{2\gamma}{\alpha}$

So, $\alpha = \frac{r}{\cos\theta}$

$h g(\rho_w - \rho_a) = \frac{2\gamma}{\alpha}$

$\Rightarrow h g(\rho_w - \rho_a) = \frac{2\gamma\cos\theta}{r}$

$\Rightarrow h = \frac{2\gamma\cos\theta}{g(\rho_w - \rho_a)}$

$\Rightarrow h = \frac{2\gamma\cos\theta}{rg(\rho_w - \rho_a)}$

$\Rightarrow h = \frac{0.15}{r} = \frac{0.3}{d}$

But

$\gamma = 72.7$ dynes/cm

$\cos\theta = 1$

$g = 9.81$ m/sec^2

$\rho_w = 1$ Mg/m^3

ρ_a = negligible

~~$P + \frac{\rho v^2}{2} + \rho g h$ = constant~~

$\frac{v^2}{2} + gz + \frac{P}{\rho}$ = constant

- Influenced by temperature, density and surface tension.
  - depends on largest pore.
- Larger the diameter of the pore → faster the water rise.
- so, faster in coarse texture.
- max^m in saturated/wet soil
- min^m in dry soil.

Water as universal solvent

- dipolar
- high dielectric constant – reduces electrical attraction of dissolved ion
- hydrogen bonding.

Viscosity

- 1 centipoise at 20°C ($\frac{1}{100}$th of a poise) 0.0089 Poise
- high viscosity due to H-bonding.
- ↑Temp → ↓viscosity

Frictional force ∝ surf area & velo. gradient

$F \propto A.\frac{dv}{dx}$ (dyne; cm^2/sec; cm)

$\Rightarrow F = \eta A.\frac{dv}{dx}$

η – Poise (coeff. of visco).

Freezing point

- Low F.D due to solutes – depression in FPD – used to characterize wilting point in the soil.

Vapour pressure

- due to dipole nature, vapour pressure is ↓.
- Saturation vapour pressure : pressure exerted by water vapour – equil^m with free and pure water

– v.p ↑ with ↑ temp and ↓ solutes/electrolytes — due to reduction of partial molar free energy of water

Vapour density = $\frac{\text{mass of } H_2O \text{ vapour}}{\text{volume of } H_2O \text{ vapour}}$

Specific humidity = $\frac{\text{mass of } H_2O \text{ vapour}}{\text{mass of air}}$

Relative humidity: degree of saturation of the atm. as aqueous vapour.

Vapour pressure deficit: vapour pressure (existing) – satur. vp. at same temperature.

Dew point: temp at which mass of air becomes saturated with the quantity of vapour.

– Schofield (1935)

$pF = 6.5 + \log[2 - RH]$

↳ log of ht of H_2O column to produce desired suction.

Freezing and thawing

↳ exothermic 80 cal/gm

↳ endothermic 80 cal/gm

– F.p ↓ with ↑ solute

↓ 1.85°C with 1 gm mole of solute in 100 gm of H_2O

↳ interference in ice like structure formation

– Schofield (1935)

$pF = 4.1 + \log$ FPD (Freezing Point Depression)

Vapourisation and condensation

↳ 590 cal/gm endothermic

↳ exothermic 590 cal/gm

– heat of evaporation at BP = 537 cal/gm

– " " sublimation = 80+590 = 670 cal/gm.

Heat capacity

- quantity of heat reqd to raise temp of a body – 1°C.
- sp. heat capacity of ice 0.49/0.5 cal/gm
  air 0.17 cal/gm

Dielectric constant

$\varepsilon = \frac{C_w}{C_a}$ — capacitance of an electrical condenser in pure H_2O / — in vacuum

- non-conductor of electricity
- capacitance – ability to store electrical energy.
- pure water ε = 78.5 at 25°C or generally 80.

Moisture potentials pF

Dry soil = > 4.5
Moist = 4.5 – 2.8
Wet = < 2.8
Saturated = 0.

Retention of water

- capillarity and adsorption
  ↓ surface tension; ↓ adhesion. — Philip F. Schofield
- Schofield (1935) – pF – express energy with which H_2O is held by the soil
  ↓ log of free energy of soil H_2O in terms of an equivalent hydraulic head.
- pF → advantage – can plot wide range of moisture conditions on one graph
  - simplify terms.
  → disadvantage – where only wet range no purpose
  - If tension = 0, log 0 = no value.

- Entire soil profile
  - Soil Water Zone / Root zone (from surface to the boundary of root zone)
  - Vadose zone (unsat) – recharging of ground water
  - Capillary fringe Zone (nearly saturated over H_2O table)

Soil Moist Constants

Saturation water content / Max^{m} retentive capacity θ_s

- soil H_2O of a disturbed soil sample of 1 cm — equil^{m} with water table.
- when all soil pores fill with water
- H_2O content of the soil when all pores - water
- matric suction - 0.
- pF = 0
- includes expanding spaces of clay minerals.
- measure by tension plate assembly
  ↳ core / sample - in contact with water column at a ht equal to middle of the sample → moisture held by soil in equi^{m} with water column → measured.
- Since all pores - filled with H_2O → $\theta_s = f$

$$\theta_s = f = \left(1 - \frac{\rho_b}{\rho_s}\right) = \left(\frac{\rho_s - \rho_b}{\rho_s}\right)$$

Field Capacity

- amt. of water held by a soil after excess H_2O - drained away and the rate of downward movement of water negligible — within 2-3 days.
- Tension - For coarse textured → 1/10th bar — pF 2. = 0.10
  - For fine textured → 1/3rd bar - pF 2.5 = 0.33
  (of potential put -ve sign)
- measuring by saturating root zone.

Permanent wilting Point

- soil wetness below which soil water extraction by plants — insufficient to meet transpir. requi.
- at which wilted plant - don't regain their turbidity
- Tension 15 bar — pF 4.2.
- Indicator plant - sunflower - Veihmeyer (FJ) and Hendrickson (AH) (1928)

- measured by pressure plate / pressure membrane apparatus (Richards, 1947)

Hygroscopic coeff

- amt of soil H_2O when an air dry soil – kept – nearly sat. atmosphere (98% RH) until it absorbs no water (equilm with the atmosphere)
- Tension 31 bar → pF 4.5
- Pressure membrane assembly for higher pressures.

Moisture equivalent

- percent. of H_2O held by 1 cm of saturated soils after – subjected to a centrifugal force of 1000 times the gravity for 30 min.
- ME = FC
- But for sand (ME < FC)
- FC = 0.gab ME + n.ib WC
- $WC = \frac{ME}{1.84}$

Factors affecting FC

- soil Texture — fineness ↑ upto silty loam then remain unchanged or increase insigni.
- soil structure – granular or crumb
- or Type of clay – expanding
- OM — increases
- Compaction – ↓
- Impeding layers – ↓.

Factors affecting WC / PWP

- All + prop. of plant – nature (root system) / stage (early stages)
  - Mesophytic survive – 10 - 25 bar
  - Xerophytic – > 25 bar
  - humid crops – < 10.

Hygroscopicity

- heat of wetting

Factors affecting HC

- nature and amount of colloids — ↑ with fineness
- temperature — ↓ as ↑ in temp as ↑ kinetic energy
- adsorbed cations — depends on vapour pressure

Low vp

- Ca-clay - more absorption than Na^+
- H > Ca > Li > Na > Ba > K. — Hycalinabapo

High vp

- Na^+ clay - more
- Li > Na > H > Ba > Ca > K. — Linahy Bacapo

Heat of wetting

- wetting - exothermic
- pF 4.5–7.0 ↳ max^m
- 0 - at hygroscopic coeff
  then increases as soil H_2O content decreases.
- max^m in oven dry soil.
- depends on OM, type of clay
- Rode Wald's equation

Soil Water classification

Briggs (1897) - lagquiet

↳ Physical — Gravitational, capillary, hygroscopic

↳ Biological — unavailable, Super available, Available

Physical

↳ Gravitational (maxm retentive cap. and FC)

↳ influence of gravity

↳ free H_2O

↳ < 0.33 bar for fine
< 0.10 bar for coarse (0.01 – 0.05) bar

↳ Capillary (continuous film around particles and capillary spaces)

0.33/0.10 bar — 31 bar

↓

Part of capillary upto 15 bar – available

↳ Hygroscopic > 31 bar (vapour form)

Biological

↳ Super available water (saturation — FC) – drainage water
– pores > 15 μ diameter
– 0 – 0.1 bar

↳ Available (WP – FC) – 15 bar – 0.1/0.3
– 4.5 – 0.1 μ diameter

↳ Unavailable H_2O – > 15 bar.

– Water availability – PWP – FC → Veihmeyer & Hendrickson (1955)

AWC for specific layer (cm)

$$Dw = \frac{AWC \times BD \times Ds}{100}$$

Ds – Thickness of soil (cm)

Dw – Depth of water in specific layer (cm)

Dp (profile) = ΣDw.

Theories of water availability

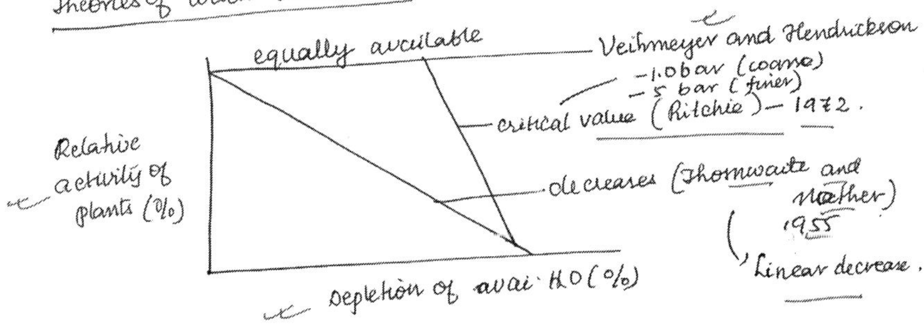

– Critical point : 60-80% depletion of available H_2O.

⇒ FC = upper limit
⇒ WP = lower limit

Main disadvan

- arbitrary values ✓
- don't consider climate and plant type. ✓

Water retention of soils

- capillarity and adsorption
  - ↳ finer
  - ↓ more imp in coarser

Second order partial differential eqn. Pierre Simon Laplace

- In soil = $h = \frac{0.279}{d} = \frac{0.3}{d}$
  ↳ capillary pores - not uniform - so air-water interfaces of various radii of curvature

- Relation of curvature of an air-H_2O interface to press. diff across interface — Laplace eqn.

$$P_b - P_a = 2\gamma\left(\frac{1}{r_1} + \frac{1}{r_2}\right)$$ — below

r_1, r_2 — principal radii of curvature above menisci

P_b — pressure of H_2O below interface
P_a — above

- mean radius (r) → +ve (when lies within H_2O phase)
  → -ve (gas phase)

Soil Moisture Characteristic Curve

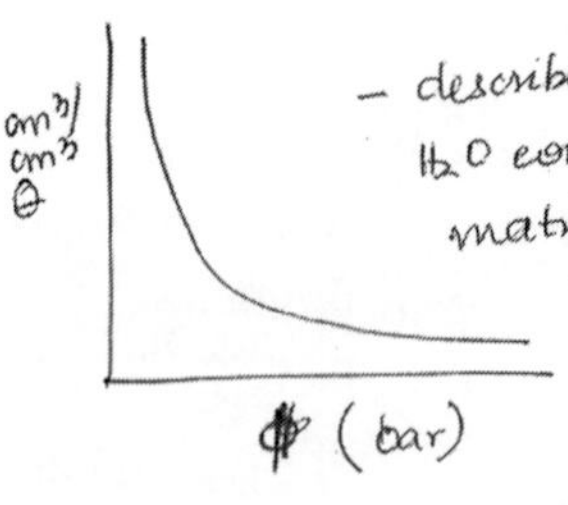

- describes functional relationship between soil H_2O content and energy status in terms of matric pot. under equilm condition
- water retention - function of suction.
  ↳ decrease with increase in suction

- rapid upto 1 bar — slow — upto 2 bar then — very slow

- saturated soil – suction/tension = 0
- With low suction → no H_2O released → so ↑ suction – until a critical value – air entry suction – H_2O released.
- first from macropores then micropores.
- Further ↑ suction → ↓ thickness of hydration envelope of H_2O.
- At low suction (0 - 1 bar) – water retention depends on capillarity – depends on pore size distribution – soil structure.
- At higher suction – water retention – depends on hydration envelope ↳ texture. ↙ specific surface.

- Disadvan
  - non linear curve – so diff. to determine matric pot. from measurement of θ or vice-versa.

Factors aff. SMCC

- soil texture ✓
- soil structure ✓
- clay minerals – mont > illite > kaolinite
- OM ✓
- compaction ✓ – decreases porosity by ↓ macropore – but amount of micropores increases – so increase in H_2O retention in intermediate (at low suction) matric suction. – But at high suction - no effect as SMCC depends on soil texture.
- soil soln ✓
  - divalent – suppression of clay

Hysteresis in SMCC

- Relationship between the two variables that changes depending on the sequences or starting point.
- desorption curve vs wetting curve

  - desorption curve: gradually drying a completely satur. soil by ↑ suction to the specified matric pot and determine θ
  - wetting curve: gradually wetting an air dry soil to the sp. matric pot. and determine θ

- Both curves - continuous but not identical.
- equilᵐ H_2O content at any matric suction > desorption

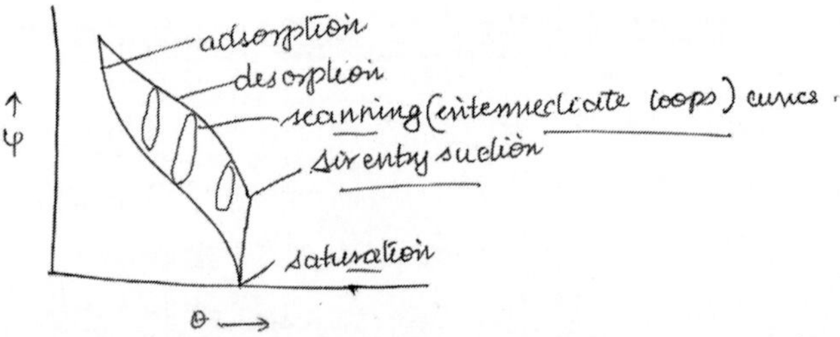

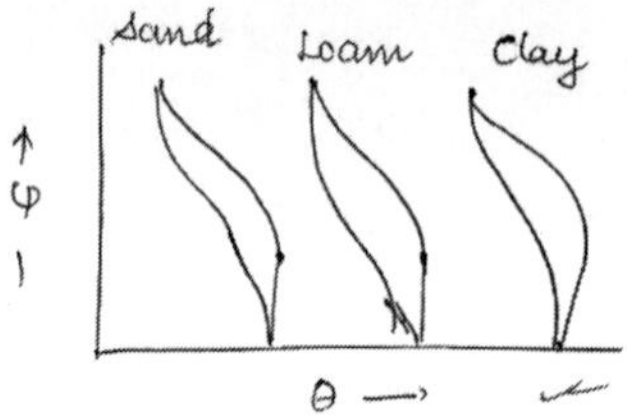

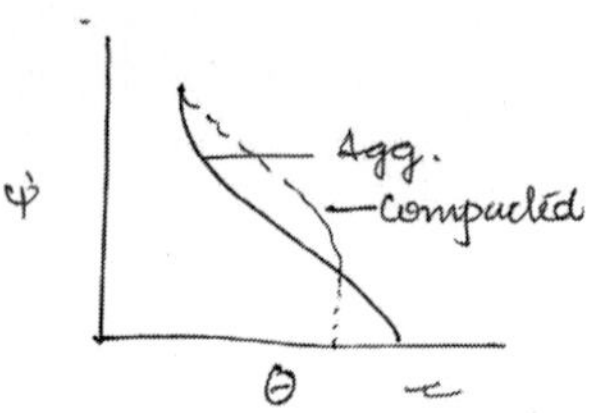

Causes of hysteresis

a) geometric nonuniformity of individual pores
- generally irregular shaped voids - interconnected by smaller passages resulting - Ink bottle effect

Ink bottle effect

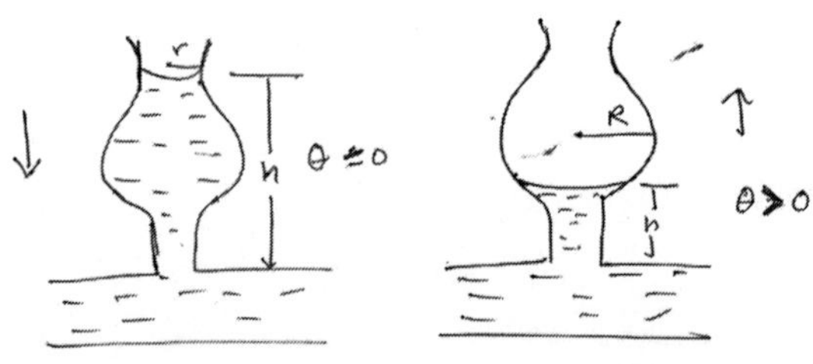

desorption ↓ depends on narrow radii of connecting channel

adsorption ↓ depends on larger pores

↓ discontinuous spurts of water called Haines jumps (after W.B Haines)

1930 → first noticed → in coarse sands.

- Hysteresis effect – more pronounced in coarse in low suction range
  ↓
  pores empty at an appreciably larger suction than that at which they fill.

b) contact angle effect

- contact angle > and so radius of curvature > in advancing menisci than receding.
- contact angle hyst – can arise due to
  - surface roughness
  - adsorption of impurities to surface.
  - mechanism of liquid mol. adsorb/desorb when interface is displaced.

c) Entrapped air
- further ↓ H_2O content of newly wetted soil.

d) swelling and shrinkage /ageing phenomenon
- results differential changes in pore space as well as pore size distribution due to change in soil structure.
- may be due to internal resistance to particle rearrangement which keeps volume higher on shrinking than on swelling.

- Inverse of slope of smcc = $\frac{d\theta}{d\phi} = \frac{d\theta}{d\phi}$ = differential (specific) water capacity

Determination of water retention charac.

- At high potential – smc – by Tension plate Assembly (fritted glass plate connected to a graduated u-type manometer fill with H_2O)
  ↓
  Place thin layer of air dry soil – over plate
  ↓
  soil saturated by maintaining H_2O level on right hand limb of manometer at par with fritted glass plate
  ↓
  Matric suction = 0.

- suction 0–15 bar – Pressure Plate apparatus – ceramic plate cell on which soil cores – saturated → + a pressure chamber in which the pressure applied — air compressor to desorb H_2O from sat. soil.

Slope of curve
- Vertical, steep — soil with large no. of pores (same size)
- Horizontal, little slope — no drainable pore in suction range
- Intermediate
  - ↳ uniform distribution of pores — uniform release of H_2O per unit change of suction.

- Potential concept of soil water — Buckingham (1907)
- " dependent on H_2O content — Gardner (1920)
- Tensiometer — measuring pot. insitu — Richards (1931)
- soil water potential
  - ↳ relative levels of potential energy in different locations within the soil — not absolute amount of potential energy.

(ISSS)

- amount of work that must be done per unit quantity of pure H_2O in order to transport reversibly and isothermally an infinitesimal quantity of H_2O from a pool of pure water at a specified elevation at atmo. pressure, to the soil H_2O.
  - ↳ reversible : no energy lost
  - isotherm : under const. temp
  - inf : so that soil H_2O remains unaffected.
- due to several forces :—
  - a) gravitational potential
  - b) matric potential
  - c) osmotic potential

- pneumatic potential (ϕ_a) = change in pressure of ambient air — Pressure membrane apparatus
- pressure potential (ϕ_p) = $\phi_m + \phi_a$ (unsaturated)

= wt of H_2O (saturated)

$$\phi_t = \phi_g + \phi_p + \phi_o$$

Scott, 2000

$$\psi_t = \psi_g + \psi_p + \psi_m + \psi_o$$

unsaturated

$$\phi_t = \phi_g + \phi_m + \phi_a + \phi_o + \ldots$$

Macroscopic level

$$\psi_t = \psi_g + \psi_p.$$

saturated

$$\phi_t = \phi_g + \phi_s + \phi_o + \ldots$$

ϕ_s = submergence potential (depends on submergence depth)

- hydraulic potential $\phi_h = \phi_g + \phi_p$
  - ↳ driving force for movement of water
- water potential $\phi_w = \phi_m + \phi_a + \phi_o$
  - ↳ ∝ to R.H of vapour in equilm with the liquid phase in soil and plant
- Overburden potential (ϕ_Ω) = when soil moves freely
  - similar to pressure pot
  - below H_2O table – ϕ_Ω part of submergence pot.
  - above H_2O table – ϕ_Ω part of matric pot.
  - difficult to separate

↳ Philips (1969)

where any addn of H_2O to the medium demands a local increase in bulk volume

↓

To describe swelling and compressible soils

↓

work performed (per unit wt of added water) against gravity and external load.

Thermodynamically – PE – diff in (partial specific free energy) between soil water and standard water

Gravitational pot

- amt of work . . . at specified elevation of the point of consider.
- effect of vertical position.
- higher the elevation, greater the ability to do work.
- strictly a field phenomenon
- independent of soil properties
- for raising – body – against gravity — ~~raised~~ work must be done — raised body store this work in the form of gravi. pot. energy.
- ϕ_g above ref point = +ve, below = –ve } However diff. of ϕ_g at 2 diff points always same

Pressure potential

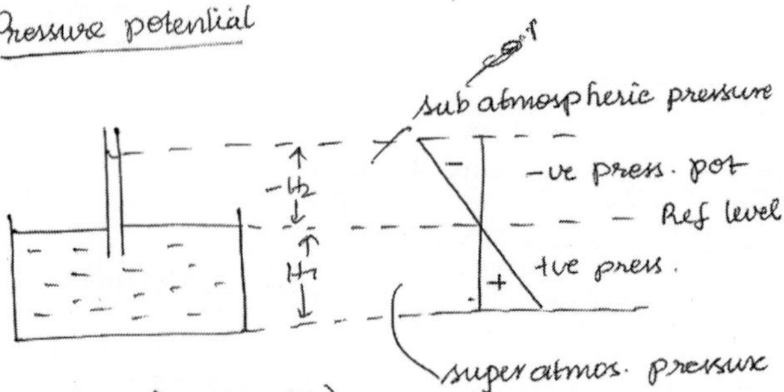

(Tensiometer)

↑ Matric potential (ϕ_m) — Sub-atm

Ref level (water Table)

↓ Submergence potential (ϕ_s) — Super-atm

(Piezometer)

- when soil water hydrostatic pressure > atm pressure – pressure pot → +ve.
- when < (subpressure commonly known as tension or suction) → -ve.
- At free surface = 0 pressure pot

matric potential

- interaction of soil water with matric.
- water in unsaturated soil - capill. & adsorption.
  - ↳ reduces energy of pure water
  - ↓ can't be separated.
  - so, work must be done
  - ↓ so pot = 0 or -ve.
- ϕ_m ↓ with ↑ in soil H_2O content
- Diff in ϕ_m in two positions.

		ϕ_m
Saturation	=	0
FC	=	-1000 mm
WC	=	-15,000 mm.

Matric suction / tension → +ve
pot → -ve.

- soil water may exhibit either -ve / +ve } → but not simultaneously

Osmotic Potential

1 cal = 4.184 J

- presence of solutes ↓ P.E
- presence of solutes ↓ vapour pressure of soil H_2O
- always negative same as matric pot.
- mayn't affect liquid flow in soil significantly
- But imp whenever a membrane or diffusion barrier present (semi-permeable membrane like soil plant root interface)

$\pi = MRT$

Osmotic pressure (dynes/cm²) — atm/bar/kPa

R — Universal Gas constant (8.314 ~~J/mol~~) J/mol k)

M — Total molar concn of solute part (mol/m³) ↳ diff to fluid

- $\phi_o = -36\, EC_e$ (EC of saturated) ← ds/m

Advantage of soil water pot

- unified measure to determine state of H_2O at any time, anywhere within soil-plant-atm continuum.
- replaces physical classification of soil water

Expressions

Mass: ergs/gm, ~~New~~ Joules/kg — L^2T^{-2} — $\frac{E}{m} = \frac{mgh}{m} = gh$ – μ – chemical potential

Volume: dynes/cm², N/m², bars, atm, KPa — $ML^{-1}T^{-2}$ — $\frac{E}{V} = \frac{mgh}{\frac{m}{\rho}} = \rho gh = \psi$ - Pressure ~~head~~ unit ↙ soil H_2O suction

Weight = h — L — Pressure head.

-ve pot. of an unsatur. soil when exp. as hydraulic head – large nos – 10^5 ~~to~~ 10^6.

So, schofield (1935) – log of -ve pressure head in cm of H_2O.

$pF = -\log h$

Conversion factors

1 dyne = 10^{-5} Newton

1 erg = 10^6 dyne·cm

1 bar = 10^6 dyne/cm^2

= 10^5 N/m^2

= 0.9869 atm

= 100 kPa

= 100 J/kg

= 14.50 lb/inch^2

= 1020 cm of water column.

1 atm = 10^6 dyne/cm^2

= 1.013 bar

= 1033 cm of H_2O column.

Measurement of soil moisture pot

- matric + grav. heads. — hydraulic heads/pot — useful in evaluating directions and magnitude of water moving forces throughout soil profile.
- matric pot — Tensiometer (in field)
  - Tension plates & air pressure extraction cells (lab)
- Total soil moist. pot → Thermocouple Psychrometer
  measuring equilm vapour pressure of soil water

Tensiometer

- provide continuous indication of soil's matric suction in-situ.
- consists of a porous cup (generally ceramic material) ~~all parts~~ ~~cont filled with water~~ connected through a tube to manometer

Refer Hillel note

steady flow:

~~Streamline~~ : when mean flow velocity $\propto$ pressure drop

streamline — Path Line

If curves are drawn for steady flow – any tangent at any point describes the direction of time average of velocity at that point

If water moving in layers, lines in which liquid part. move in time t.

Laminar flow : when adjacent layers of water moving in parallel layers of streamline/pathline in diff. velocities — slide over each other without intersection

Turburlent flow mean flow velocity is not $\propto$ press. drop.

- Refer Darcy's Law from Hillel.

Assumptions of Darcy's Law — 9 assumptions

- negligible K.E of H_2O – when flow vel. small as compared to PE
- constant mass density of H_2O } valid as long as temp doesn't change
- constant viscosity of H_2O }
- streamline flow – when flow vel Critical velocity. (As flow vel ↑ – turbulent)
- Re < 1
- porous medium
- no attraction between fluid and the medium
- isothermal
- fluid be incompressible.

iv) Intensive tillage – affecting SOC – breakdown of aggregates

v) Population pressure

II

Types of soil erosion (water) (5)

– Splash erosion

– raindrop impact – on exposed or bare soil – first stage in erosion – dispersing soil aggregates.

– can rise as high as 0.7 m above the ground and transport horizontally – 1.5 m

– results in formation of surface crusts → ↓ infiltration – ↑ runoff. → germination hampered → if germ → crop stand poor.

– falling rain drop – generate force – 14 times of its wt.

– Produces 3 effects :–

a) beating action

b) detachment

c) displacement

– sheet erosion

– uniform removal of soil layers from sloping lands.

– soil matrix lost. but remain undetected – long period

– thin veneer of soil – removed from large areas uniformly.

+

stream Bank erosion

– fast moving water – ↑K.E cut deeper under the stream banks as a conseq. of increased peak flow.

– Stream banks erode either by

– runoff flowing over the side of the stream bank

– scouring /undercutting ~~effect of~~ below ~~to~~ the H_2O surface.

– results in ↑ sediments, suspended mat in streams and rivers –

– rivers change their courses ~~a~~ – leading to flash floods during high intensity rains.

Mass movement and landslides

- in response to the force of gravity accompanied by the removal of forests and construction of hill roads.
- Mass movements :- slumping, soil creep, rotational slope, rockfall, rockslide and mudslide.
- Landslide: outward and downward movement of slope forming mat. composed of natural rocks, soil, artificial fills etc.

Specialized forms of water erosion

Soil Organic matter

- SOM - consists of a complex system of substances ranging from components of org. residues of plants and animals undergoing decomposition, metabolic products of microbes, ~~seco~~ products of secondary synthesis and humic substances.

- Influence on soil fertility

CPNC TMB

- soil colour - warming
- physical conditions of the soil
- reservoir of nutrient - prevents leaching of elements - CEC > 300 cmol(p+)/kg
- clay-complexes with OM - increase buffering and exchange capacity of the soil.
- reduces toxicity of metals - stable complexes.
- N, P, S and micronutrients - available through mineralization
- biodegradation of fungicides, pesticides and herbicides.

Carbon/nitrogen/P/S ratios and Plant nut.

- 1% OC - in coarse sand to 3.5% in grassland.
- C:N of an ideal soil: 10:1 - 12:1
- nutrients and OM interactions - upon degradation of plant and animal residues - microbial biomass.

- Org. N, P, S $\underset{Imm}{\overset{Min}{\rightleftharpoons}}$ NH_4^+, PO_4^{3-}, SO_4^{2-}

- C/N/P/S ratio in soil humus = 140 : 10 : 1.3 : 1.3 - although variations in diff. soils.
- C:N - legumes and green young leaves - 10:1 - 30:1
  - sawdust - 600:1
  - microbes - 5:1 - 10:1 (Bacteria, act - 5:1; Fungi - 10:1.)
  - cultivated soil - 8:1 - 15:1
- C:N ratio lower in subsurface.

- when wider C:N ratio – competition among m/o and plants
- depe maintainace of SOC is dependent on level of nitrogen.
- wider C:N ratio — heterotrophic m/o – active – proliferate — nitrate level ↓ as they utilise native soil nitrogen — so basal appln of nitrogen through inorg. fert.

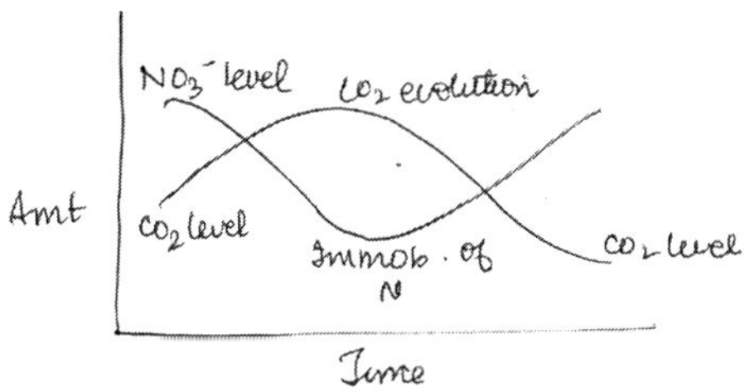

- high/wider C/N, C/P, C/S ratios favour net immobi. followed by net mineral. at later stage.
- diff. in release of N, P, S from SOM – due to
  a) release of N, P, S doesn't occur in required ratios
    ↳ as present in diff. org. compounds
    ↳ degradability diff.
  b) some losses or fixed.
  c) C/N, C/P, C/S regulate net min/immob.

ⓒ ✓ Carbon stocks in Indian soils

- Low content in Indian soils due to :—
  a) excessive tillage
  b) imbalanced use of fert.
  c) removal of crop residues from field
  d) severe soil degradation
  e) prevalence of humi. trop. sub-trop, ~~and arid~~ arid and semi arid climatic conditions.

- SOC high – UIA – Vertisols, Inceptisols and Alfisols.
- SIC high – Aridisols.
- Arid climate (low annual rainfall < 500 mm)
- soil organic carbon – min^m – Mollisol
  max^m – Alfisols.
  - min^m – Brown forest soils
  - max^m – Alluvial soils.

@ ✓ Estimation of soil organic matter

- Rapid titration method (walkley and Black, 1934)
- known amount of soil – oxidized with a mix. of $K_2Cr_2O_7$ and H_2SO_4
  ↳ utilizing heat of dilution — Unused $K_2Cr_2O_7$ back titrated with ferrous sulphate $FeSO_4 \cdot 7H_2O$ or ferrous amm. sulphate $FeSO_4 \cdot (NH_4)_2SO_4 \cdot 6H_2O$

- SOM = SOC × 1.724
  ↳ Van Bemmelen factor as organic matter contains 58% of carbon → 100/58 = 1.724.

- Interpretation (%)
  - < 0.5 – Low
  - 0.5–0.75 – Med
  - > 0.75 – High.

@ Constituents of soil Organic matter

- plant tissues and animal and waste products of animals.
  ↳ cellulose, hemicellulose, protein, lignin etc.
- Decomposition of org. compounds results in —
  a) Production of CO_2, water, energy and biomass
  b) Mineralization of N, P, S in inorg. form.
  c) Formation of resist. mat.
- Most C – as CO_2 return to atmosphere but 1/3rd remains in soil
  - as living org (5%)
  - as humus (25%)

60-80% as CO_2
↑
Organic Residues
- Biomass (soil org) — 3-8%
- non humic comp — 3-8%
- complex humic sub — 10-30%

% distribution of diff. components

non-humic	usual range (% by wt)
Lipids	1-6%
Carbohydrates	5-25%
Proteins/peptides/amino ā	9-16%
Others	traces.
humic	80%

10-15%

85-90%

non humic	humic
- less	- more percent
- more well defined chemically and are usually coloured	- i) percentage ii) polyme iii) persistance iv) molecular wt v) stability
- simple, low mol. wt comp.	-
- transcient existence in soils.	- not only in soils - marines and lake sediments, peat bogs, composts, sewage etc.
- ~~used~~ (	

- Total C in earth as humic acids - 550 Pg > land biomass carbon (480 Pg)

Pools of SOM

- varies seasonally
- dependent on various factors such as soil type, veg and climate
- concept of pools: based on their susceptibility to microbial decomposition and longevity.

8 pools

LLMF BWSE.

a) Litter
- macro-org. matter such as crop residues - lie on crop surface.

b) Light fraction
- org. residues in various stages of decomposition.
- Root residues.
- indicator of changes in labile org. matter as affected by tillage, cropping practices and envn. factors

c) Microbial biomass
- 2% of total soil C.
- 2 roles — agents of degradation / labile pool of nutrients

d) Faunal Biomass
- less studied
- But earthworms

e) Belowground Plant constituents
- such as roots

f) water - soluble organics
- in view of plant nutrition and envn (metal ion toxicities through chelation)

g) stable humus
- bulk of SOM

h) soil enzymes -
- quantitatively minute
- all biochemical reactions dependent on them.
- Dehydrogenase activ. - related to quantity of decomposible OM.

@ Extraction and Fractionation

- SOM
  - fulvic acid - ~~both~~ soluble in both acid & alkali.
  - humic ā - soluble in alkali
  - humin - insoluble

Other fractions -

a) hymatomelanic ā

b) gray and brown humic ā

- FA, HA and humin - are not the compds of a definite comp - but group of compounds having similar solubility characteristics

- Humus of mollisol - richer in HA
- Spodosol - FA
- Vertisol - humin

Reagents for extraction

efficiency

Humic subs

- ↳ strong bases
  - NaOH — 80%
  - Na_2CO_3 — 30%
- ↳ neutral salts - $Na_4P_2O_7$, NaF — 30%
- ↳ acid salts — 30%
- ↳ organic chelates — Formic ā (HCOOH) - 55%

Hydrolyzable compds

- Amino ā — Hot-6 N HCl — 25-45
- Sugars — Hot 1N H_2SO_4 — 5-25
- Polysaccharides — NaOH, hot water — <5%
- Clay bound biochemicals — ~~HF~~ — 5-50%
- free biochemicals (amino ā, sugars) — H_2O, 80% alchol. — 1%
- Fats, waxes, resins — usual fat solvents — 2-6%

Fractionation

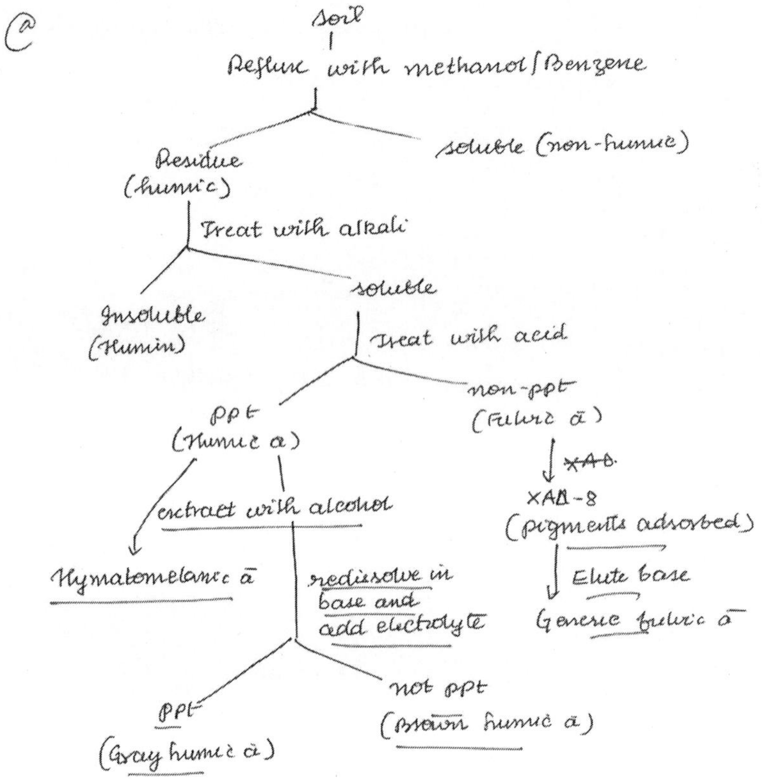

Humin

- may consist of humic acids so intimately bound to mineral matter – can't be separated –
- may have highly condensed humic matter with ↑ C content (>6%) – so insoluble in alkali
- also may contain fungal melanins.

Humic ā

- ppt under acidic condition.
- Crude humic ā – from grassland soils – ↑ ash content – >30% –
  ↳ reduction of ash content – by repeated ppt. with mineral ā and by passage through ion-exchange resins.

- To remove clay— high speed centrifugation after re-dissol. humic ā in a dilute alkali and adjusting pH -7.0
- For humic ā with low ash content — treated -with ā solutions containing (HF).
  - ↳ reduce ash content — by dissolving hydrated clay minerals &
  - form complexes with di or trivalent cations.
- crude humic ā mat
  ↓
  dissolve in base
  ↓
  Ionic strength adjusted to 0.1 M (wrt KCl)
  ↓
  sample centrifuged to remove clay
  ↓
  acidified to ppt → sample several treatments with dilute acid - 0.3 N HF : 0.1 N HCl
  ↓
  dialyzed against DW
  ↓
  freeze dried

Metal — New
Clay — centrifuge.

- To remove metal ions - sample-dialyzed in presence of cation exc. resin in H^+ form.
- Reduction in ash content- may be accompanied by loss of humic matter - by liberation of low mol wt fulvic ā bound to unpurified humic ā through metal linkage.

Fulvic ā

- acid filtrate - after removal of humic ā - dialyzed extensively against DW.
- non-dialyzable part consists of
  - fulvic ā
  - polysaccharides
  - proteinaceous constituents

  } → Both are passed through a column of XAD-8 →
- dialysate — contains fulvic ā as well as amino ā, sugars

- For the dialysate— all the dark coloured om- retained by resin
  - Others pass through and removed in effluent

Characterization of humic substances and Techniques

a) Elemental composition

- major elements C and O

	Humic acids	Fulvic acids
Carbon —	50-60% ↑	40-50%
Oxygen —	30-35%	45-50% ↑

(Stevenson, 1994)

b) Functional groups

- Both contain large no. of a func. groups — impart ability to form complexes with metal ions — contribute to pH-dependent CEC to soil.
- Principal ones- carboxylic (COOH)
  - phenolic OH
  - enolic OH
  - quinine
  - hydroxyquinone
  - alcoholic OH.

- Fulvic a.- more density of oxygen containing functional groups.

	Humic a.	cmol(p+)kg-1	Fulv. acid
Total acidity	560 – 890 500 – 900		640 – 1420 900 – 1400
COOH	150 – 570		520 – 1120.

(Stevenson, 1991)

c) Spectroscopic approaches — UV-visible – quantitative
 — IR — qualitative vibration of f.g.

- spect. measurement in diff. regions of EM spectrum
- advantages -
  - non destructive
  - small sample wt. required
  - experimentally simple
  - don't require any special manipulative skills.

d) E_4/E_6 ratio

- ratio of absorbances in 465 and 665 nm
- for characterization purposes
- Ratio for humic ā → < 5.0 → HA — 3-5
  fulvic ā → 6.0-8.5 FA — 6-9.

- Procedure

  2-4 mg of FA/HA
  ↓
  10 ml of 0.05 $NaHCO_3$
  (which gives opt pH for absorbance measu)

- ratio ↓ with ↑ mol wt
- index (inverse) of humification
- ↑ → ↑ aliphatic structures.

→ Inverse relationship $E_4/E_6 \frac{1}{\alpha}$ MRT (mean residence time) &

e) ~~Adso~~ Absorption spectroscopy

- Absorption in UV (200-400 nm) / visible (400-800 nm) } → caused by atomic and electrometric vibrations and involves excitation of e^- from ground state to higher energy levels.

- compds containing ~~unpaired~~ unbounded e^- on O and S atoms – capable of showing absorption.

- Infrared spec – provides information – on nature, reactivity and structural arrangement of oxygen-containing functional groups, the occurence of protein and carbohydrate constituent and presence/absence of inorg. impurities.

- Infrared – also studies org-metal and org. pesticide interaction.

f) Colour producing groups

- Part of org. molecule responsible for producing colour — chromophore or chromophoric g — responsible for dark colour — haven't been established but a combination of several structural type is suspected.

g) Colloidal Properties of Humic substances

- colloidal state — condition intermediate between true soln (ionic or molecular dimension) and particulate suspension
- colloidal range — 0.001 to 1.0 µm in diameter — corresponds to particles ranging from 10^{-6} to 10^{-3} mm.

@ Structural components of HA and FA

- Kononova (1966) - HA
- Schnitzer (1972) - FA
- chromatographic patterns of degradation products - fingerprint
- occurence of phenolic aldehyles in degradation prod. — indicator of terestrial org. matter in ocean sediments — presence of resorcinol derivatives.

Organic - Metallic Interaction

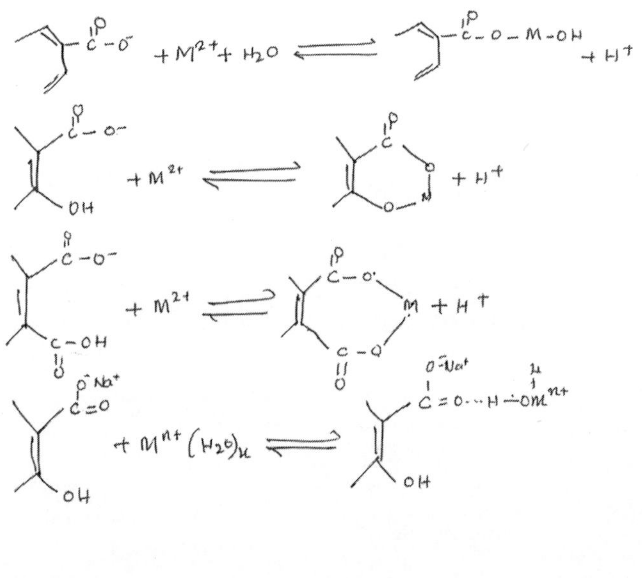

- monovalent cations (Na^+, K^+) – cation exch. reactions – through formation of salts with carbonyl groups as ~~COO~~ R-COO^-Na^+, RCOO^-K^+ electrovalent

- Multivalent cations – forming coordinate linkages with org. molecules. co-ordinate

- Metal-org complexes influence on soil @

  - org. subs – involved in weathering – serve as agents for transport of sesquioxides in leached ~~ter~~ terrestrial soils – notably spodosol.

  - carriers of trace elements – complex ~~of~~ of trace elem with FA → also water soluble.

  - availability of ~~P~~ insoluble mineral phosphate P – through complexation of Fe and Al – acid
    Ca – calcaf.

  - reduced metal ion concn – toxic level.

  - ~~of~~ polyvalent cations – linkage – humic sub and clay – affecting physical prop. of soil.

  - acts as buffer in ameliorating adverse effects of toxic heavy metals.

- Humic sub – forms complexes with trace elements
  - soluble
  - Insoluble → naturally insoluble due to interaction with clay mineral.

- FA – less susceptible to ppt than humic a due to
  - ↳ because of lower mole. wt –
  - ↳ higher contents of acidic func. groups.

- when HA and FA dissolve in water – dissociation of acidic functional groups occurs R-COOH = R-COO^- + H^+. – molecule assumes a stretched configuration due to repulsion of charged groups.

- When metal ions - added - charge reduced - through salt formation and molecule collapse — ↓ solubility.
- Polyvalent cations — link individual mol. together to produce chain like structures.
- Metal complexes of humic ā — soluble at low metal humic ā ratios — but when ↑ metal conc — ppt occurs as chain like structure. — and isolated COOH groups - neutralized through salt bridges.
- Mechanisms - affecting solubility of humic substances in presence of polyvalent cations —

  a) precipitation - due to protonation - ↓ charge on humic polymes.

  b) formation of hydroxy complexes of metal ions at high pH

  c) Formation of chain like structure through metal ion bridge.

  d) attachment to the clay particle and oxide surfaces through metal ion linkage.

- Approaches to determine —

  Binding capacity — proton release, metal ion retention as determined by competition with a cation exc. resin and dialysis.

  Binding sites — UV and fluorescence spectroscopy.

- Factors affecting quantity of metal ions bound —
  - pH ↑
  - amount and kind of acidic f.g ↑
  - ionic strength ↓
  - mol. wt. ↑
- Trivalent cations bound in greater amounts. ↑
- Divalent ones — strongest ~~complexation~~ coordination complexes (eg Cu^{2+})
  — form weak complexes (Zn^{2+}, Mn^{2+})

- Imp charact - stability constant -

(c) Organic matter with Pesticides

- Sorption of pest. on humic a — inhibits their transport
- Binding — original pest. / or its transformation prod } — caused by abiotic and biotic agents
- As FA more soluble than HA —,
  ↳ so special function in pest. transf —
  - a) act as transporting agents for certain pesticides in soils and natural water - soluble humic sub act as carriers of xenobiotics in aquatic env. (transport)
  - b) fulvic a - by their ↑ func. g — catalyze chemical decomp. of herbicides. (↑ f-g catalyze chemical dec)
- Binding of pest. to om — sorption (Vander Waals force), H- bonding, hydrophobic bonding, electrostatic interactions, covalent bond, or combinations.
- HA and FA from same sources — diff. effects on adsorption of pest — adsorption on soil treated by HA → ↑ than FA.

Clay - Org. complexes

- Colloidal clay and org. fractions — don't exist in pure form — form stable clay-org. complexes.
- exert a profound influence on soil env - by controlling phy. che and bio prop.
  ↳ aeration, porosity, etc.
- Adsorption - determined by - prop. of org. mol.
  - pH
  - kind and amt of clay

- nature of exc. cations on clay surface.

- Org. substances – protected – against attack by m/o. ↑ mutual ↓
- org. subs – cement soil part – aggregation
- Humic subs – retain w by clay minerals – 2 ways: –

a) attachment to clay surfaces – through cation and anion exch, bridging by polyvalent cations, H bonding, Vander-

c) penetration into interlayer spaces of expanding type of clay minerals.

- Org. matter – role in cohesion of clay and/or clay-humic complexes into larger part – such as by sharing of inter-crystalline ionic forces between clay part or by bridging through the action of polyvalent cations and humus.

- Clay – principal binding agent in soil – OM don't have capacity to hold the soil particles primarily – but to modify the forces through which clay part. themselves are attracted to one another.

@ Management of soil OM for sustainable Ag

- Organic carbon – 9.55 Pg
- Inorganic carbon – 4.14 Pg.

i) conservation tillage
ii) Cover crops
iii) crop rotation
iv) crop residues
v) Nutrient managem. – ↑ SOC @ 50 - 150 kg $ha^{-1} yr^{-1}$
vi) Org. amendments

5000 kg FYM (2.23 t ha^{-1})

↳ B – 0.1 kg
Mn – 1.
Co – 0.005
Cu – 0.08
Zn – 0.48
Mo – 0.01

vii) Commercial humates
- derived from lignites
- mixed lignites, ammonium humate fert
- expensive.

Chemistry of Potassium Fixation in soil

- when some mica clay particles – put in a soln of very low K concn containing ↑ concn of other ions – K^+ will be released slowly – from in-between the adjacent layers of mica at its broken edges, causing ↑ in spacing between layers – to allow larger hydrated cations such as Ca, Na to enter ⟶ K release

- ↳ partially reversible because if clay-depleted of K^+ (non-exch) – put in a ~~solution~~ concentrated K soln ⟶ proportion K – enter interlayer by replacing hydrated other cations – make two adjacent layers come closer and strip K^+ ion of its hydration shell – lock it into 'ditrigonal cavity' – nearly a dimension equal to that of unhydrated K^+ ion.

- Release and fixation – concn-dependent
- Potass. release – soln K concn below Release Threshold Level.
- " fixation – " " " above Fixation Tr. " " "
- Two opposing forces involved in fixation
  - a) force of attraction between two -vely charged adjacent layers
  - b) opposing hydration force of K^+ ion to retain its hydration shell.

- Dioctahedral mica – Muscovite – fixes more K than trioctahedral mica – phlogopite and biotite
  - ↳ because more tetrahedral rotation – so less K-O distance

- Vermiculite and montmorillonite also fixes.
  - Vermiculite ↓ both wet and dry conditions
  - Montmorillonite ↳ only dry (as layer charge of mont. not sufficient enough to strip potassium off the hydration shell under moist cond).

- Similarly to K^+ ⟶ ↑ concn of soln NH_4^+ – fixation – making adjacent layers collapse and block release of any non-exch cations from interlayer space – therefore –

Therefore, higher concn of NH_4^+ (1 N Neutral Ammonium acetate) – used to extract cations – exchangeable.

- If other cations like Ca^{2+}, Na^+ – used to extract exc. cations – chances of extracting non-exch cations – by opening up the layers – overestimating.

Phosphate fixation in soil

- combination of chemical processes – by which a portion of avai. P becomes non-available.
- Two ways –

a) Transformation of adsorbed phase.

- Change of configuration of adsorbed phosphate with time
- Phosp. freshly adsorbed on colloid surface – by ligand exc. mechanism – assumes a monodentate configuration.
- with time, – slow reaction continues –

↓ adsorbed phosp forms another linkage to it through other OH-group

↓ establish more stable bidentate config.

↓ P gets fixed.

(→ replacement of one surface-OH grp by one ortho-phosphate ion)

- This transformation takes place even at low P conc in soil soln – but takes time.

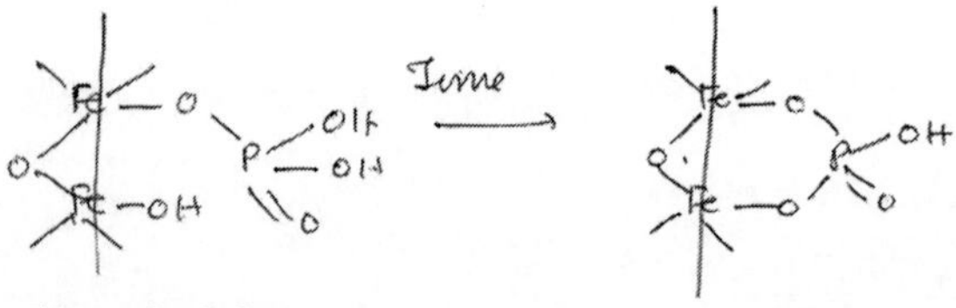

Monodentate Bidentate

- surface precipitation

when
- concⁿ of P soil solution ↑ — more adsorption — surface —
- when all adsorbed P concentrates on the surface — initiating the nucleation of aluminium Phosphate or iron phosphate on clay surface — result in formation of full-fledged ppt — which may subsequently form a separate phase, crystallize and becomes less available.

b) Precipitation in soil solution following solubility Product principles.

- SP - defined as product of activities (or concⁿ - if solⁿ very dilute) of the constituent ions in solⁿ of a sparingly soluble salt at equilibrium — constant at particular temp.

eg. Dissociation of TCP yields

$$Ca_3(PO_4)_2 \rightarrow 3Ca^{2+} + 2PO_4^{3-}$$

Equilibrium constant (K_{sp}) also called SP.

$$(Ca^{2+}) \times (Ca^{2+}) \times (Ca^{2+}) \times (PO_4^{3-}) \times (PO_4^{3-}) = K_{sp}.$$

- Three situations wrt to experimentally determined Ionic activity product (IAP) of a sparingly soluble TCP

If ~~TCP < IAP~~ IAP < K_{sp} = unsaturated

IAP = K_{sp} = saturated

IAP > K_{sp} = supersaturated

- solubility product principle - If IAP exceeds SP → ppt formation
- when a granule of soluble P compounds like SSP, DAP added to soil — absorbs moisture - water soluble P dissolves in it — producing ↑ concⁿ of P solution having very low pH (↳ SSP) or high pH (↳ DAP) — reacts with surrounding Al or Ca - depending on pH

- ↑ concn of phosphate > SP of Al phosphate or Ca phosphate around or at site of appln → ppt of P → P concn soln ↓
- But irrigation and IAP < K_{sp} → ppt will dissolve – P avail ↑.
- This ppt with time – crystallizes – solubility ↓.
- Thus – in acid soils – varuscite (Al-P) strengite (Fe-P) – form as fert reaction products
- alkaline – DCP – OCP – TCP – finally apatite

Relationship with pH and Phosphate fixation

Acid soil

- Al and Fe control the solubility
- source of Al in acid soil is $Al(OH)_3$ – most soluble among sparingly soluble salts of Al.
- With ↓ pH → H^+ ion activity ↑ and OH^- activity ↓ ~~because~~
- To make Ksp ~~con~~ of $Al(OH)_3$ constant – Al^{3+} ion concn ↑ with ↓pH
- Al^{3+} ion – also in equilm with $AlPO_4$.
- So, if Al^{3+} ion activity ↑ → PO_4^{3-} ion activity ↓ by forming ppt ($AlPO_4$) so as to keep Ksp of $AlPO_4$ constant.

Alkaline or neutral soils

- Ca ion – control solubility of P.
- $CaHPO_4$ (dicalcium phosphate) – most soluble.

Non-calcareous

- assume a constant concn of Ca of ~~10^{-2.5}~~ $10^{-2.5}$ moles/L
- Since Ca activity constant – ppt will depend upon the activity of HPO_4^{2-} ion.
- with ↑ pH, HPO_4^{2-} ion concn ↑ and when it exceeds Ksp. with Ca ion activity – P ↑ ppt and ↓ P soln.

Calcareous soil

- Ca ion activity - not constant - but decreases with rise in pH because CO_3^{2-} activity increases with pH and when Ksp > — forms ppt as $CaCO_3$.
- Thus, due to ↓ Ca ion activity - P ion activity ↑ to keep Ksp of Ca-P constant.
- Thus, P fixation ↓ with increase in soil pH in calcareous soil.

E value :-

- direct application of isotopic dilution ~~technique~~ principle.
- amt of nut. in soil at equilm with the same nut in soil solution can be measured with E value.

$$\text{Surface}\ ^{31}P + \text{solution}\ ^{32}P \rightleftharpoons \text{surface}\ ^{32}P + \text{soln}\ ^{31}P$$

At equilm

$$\frac{\text{surf}\ ^{31}P}{\text{surf}\ ^{32}P} = \frac{\text{soln}\ ^{31}P}{\text{soln}\ ^{32}P}$$

- possible to measure both capacity and intensity factors of same sample.
- represents labile form of nut.
- ,, total amt of nut undergoing isotopic dilution.
- Russels, Erickson and Adams

A-value

- Fried and Dean (1952)
- when plant is confronted with two sources of a given nut - plant will absorb from each of these in proportion to respective amounts available.
- amount of available nut in soil to be determined in terms of fert. standard is known as A value.

$$A = \frac{B(1-Y)}{Y}$$

B — amt. of applied fert nut

Y — Prop. of nut in the plant derived from fert nut.

A — Amt. of available nut. in soil

Pdff — % of total P in plant derived from fert.

$$A\ \text{value} = \left[\frac{\%\ \text{Pdfs}}{\%\ \text{Pdff}}\right] \times \text{rate of P appln (kg/ha)}$$

$$\%\ \text{Pdfs} = 100 - \%\ \text{Pdff}.$$

L-value= Larsen (1952)

- If labelled fertilizer phos. is added to soil at diff. levels or rates and plants are grown, the specific activity analysis of the plant mat. gives a constant value which is attributable to the equilm between the applied P and exc. P in soil
- amt so determined is known as L value and also termed as Labile form of phosphorus.

$$L \text{ value} = \left[\left(\frac{a_o}{a_p}\right) - 1\right] \times \text{Applied fert P}$$

L value = amt of P in soil and soil soln which is exchangeable with added P to soil as measured by a plant growing in the system.

- Gibbs Free Energy $\Delta G = H - TS$
- colloids - Grahams.
- Toricelli's – $v = \sqrt{2gz}$
- Bernoulli's – $z + \frac{v^2}{2g} + \frac{P}{\rho_w g} = \text{constant}$
- Poiseuille's – $q = \frac{\pi r^4}{8\eta}\left(\frac{\Delta P}{L}\right)$

- Beer's Lambert's Law: ~~OD = log T~~ log $\frac{\text{Transmitted intensity}}{\text{Incident}}$

Absorbance (OD) $= 2 - \log(\%T)$

$= -\log\left(\frac{\%T}{100}\right)$

- Avogadro's no: 6.023×10^{23}
- Not a potash bearing mineral:— Muscovite, Feldspar, Olivine, Biotite
- enantiomers:- optical isomer: mirror images — non-superposable
- Isomers:— each of two or more compds— same formula but different arrangement of atoms (diff. properties).
- Isotopes: atoms with same no. of protons but diff. neutrons.
  - same atomic no but diff mass no.
- Calcareous soil: deficient in Zn, Fe.
  : Boron deficiency
- Organometallic complex — Metal ion — Lewis acid — accept an electron. / Org — ligand
- C axis of smectite :— 1.40 nm.
- If nitrate formation in soil independent of amt of ammo N — zero order reaction.
  ↳ independent of concn of reactants
- Mo:— fixed on same sites on soil colloids as Phosphate
- pH of calcareous soil in equilm with atmos CO_2 — 8.8/7.5/8.2/8.5 ✓
- Molarity of concentrated H_2SO_4:— 18.4. — 98%.
  Perchloric: 11.6 — 70%
  H_3PO_4: 15.2 — 85%
  NaOH: 17.6 — 47%
- agroecological subregions in India: NBSS & LUP: ~~50~~ 60
- ICAR (NARP) (NREP) :. — 127 agro-climatic ~~NREP~~
- NBSS — regions: 20.
- Dehydrogenase activity : respiration
- Actinomycetes: — later stage of composting

- rhizosphere: Gram -ve, non spore forming
- $AR^K : \frac{[K^+]}{\sqrt{[Ca^{2+} + Mg^{2+}]}}$
- size of micro-watershed:

  sub - 10,000 - 50,000 ha
  mille - 1000, 10,000
  micro - 100-1000
  mini - 10-100

- soil test based fert recom. for targeted yield of crops - India: - B. Ramamoorthy.
- errors - minm - made at wavelength of maxm adsorpt.
- Chlorites: - Phyllosilicates
- Montmorillonite: external surf area: 60-120 m^2/g
- Comm. in soil science & Plant analysis. - Francis & Taylor
- measured concn of ion ≠ actual concn in soil due to complexation and ion pair
- Quatering: bulk sample to desired quantity
- double ring infiltrometer: - minimizes horiz. flow.
- Biogas - India: SV Desai - anaero
- Real time N management: - plant demand
- Formulas of soil/plant Test
- ease of miner: - urea > aminosugars > protein > amino ā > humified N) nucleic ā
- EBT: Gypsum req.
- Anion exch. : ↑ kaolinite
- nitrification → -3 to +5

- BIOLOG :- Microbial identification
- half life of ^{14}C : 5730 years.
- Karl Fisher :- moist-determ. in urea.
- EBT : Ca est
- Ascorbic a: ~~Available~~ P det.
- Alkaline perm : Av. N.
- Grigg's reagent : Mo. est.
- Ligand exchange : most imp determinant CEC/AEC/pH/ion mix
- CEC of laterites < 16.
- Desert soils : Aridisols, Entisol.
- Kjeldahl digestion: K_2SO_4 :- ↑ boiling point of medium. (temp)

  : catalyst :- HgO. or $CuSO_4$
- nanoparticles : 1 nm-100nm.
- Bentonite. - montmo.
- Karl fisher . pyridine containing fert
- Basic slag
- Leaching requirements - Richards
- nernst eqn: $E = E^0 + \frac{RT}{F} \ln \frac{Oxd}{Red}$.

  $= E^0 + \frac{0.059}{n} \log \frac{Oxd}{Red}$.
- ppt indicator :- Orthophenanthroline ~~starch~~ : redox reactions.

  ~~murexide~~ : metal indicator

  Starch :- ppt. indicator

  ferric alum : adsorption.
- Mo-Fe (high molecular) — dinitrogenase — because N binds to the protein moiety

  Fe (lower). — dinitrogen reductase - since second moiety serves function of reduction of ~~Fe~~ Mo-Fe protein

Org C

Volume of 1 N $K_2Cr_2O_7$ used = 0.5 × (B − S)

$$\% \text{ org C in soil} = \frac{0.5 \times (B - S) \times 0.003 \times 100}{W}$$

Avail. N

- volume of N/50 NaOH used (titrate value) = X ml.
- ~~vol. of N/50 acid used~~. or → vol of H_2SO_4 taken.
- $\% \text{ of avail N} = \frac{(25 - x) \times 0.00028 \times 100}{W}$

Bray I :— 1:10 Mehlich - I : 0.05 N HCl + 0.025 N H_2SO_4 (pH 1.2) 1:4

Bray II :— 1:20

Morgan's — 10 ml of glacial acetic in 1 litre of 0.5% NaOH — pH 8.4 − 1:5

Bray

= A × 50 ppm

Olsen

= A × 100 ppm

Ammonium acetate K

Avail K = C × 5 when (1:5) 5 gm : 25 ml.

Ca

meq of Ca+Mg in V_1 ml of aliquot = $(V_2 - V_3)$ ml.

meq of Ca+Mg in V ml of extract = $(V_2 - V_3) \times 0.01 \times \frac{V}{V_1}$

(V_2: EDTA volume (titre value); V_3: EDTA blank; 0.01: Normality of EDTA; V_1: volume of aliquot used.)

meq of . . . . /100 gm of soil = $(V_2 - V_3) \times 0.01 \times \frac{V}{V_1} \times \frac{100}{W}$

meq of Ca /100 gm = $(V_2 - V_3) \times 0.01 \times \frac{V}{V_1} \times \frac{100}{W}$

meq of Mg = −

S

Available S (ppm) = C×6.25

DTPA

Available heavy metal (ppm) = (C - C₀) × 2 — blank; dilution factor

- Total land degradation in India : 187.8 M ha
- Solodization: removal of alkali.
- Tri acid - not for N, S.
- Vertical mulching / self mulching - Ver Black soils
- Humus ppt : 4.8
- Micas - isom. subs - predom - octahedral
- available P - but not plants - E.
  L - crops.
- Wavelength of solar radiation - 0.5 μm.
- concn of pure H_2O : 55.5 mol/L.
- Sheet erosion ; Red & Black.
- Albite & Anorthite - identify - Zoning.
- First National Forest Policy - 1952
- About 50% of atm is upto 5-6 km from earth.
- Cd toxicity - Kidney.
- International Agroforestry Org. - Nairobi, Kenya.
- Albedo of earth :- 30%.
- Partly soluble in H_2O - CAN.
- Father of agri meteorology - LA Ramdas.
- Legumes : NPK : 1:2:2
- Nalgonda technique - Fluoride.
- WMO - Geneva.
- pF upper Plastic Limit : 0.5

Journal of 'Plant & Soil' — Netherlands.

1 ha cm of H_2O = 100 tonnes H_2O
100,000 litres H_2O

- First step in wind erosion: suspension.
- High temp in ICPAES – Plasma.
- Leaf N analysis :- Na_2SO_4 / K_2SO_4 and $CuSO_4 \cdot 5H_2O$ in ratio of 20:1.

SiO_4
- Posonicdo >>>.
- 1 meq of HCl = 14mg of N.
- Acetylene – 2600–2800°C Flame Photometer.
- 1 mg of H^+ = 20 mg of Ca^{2+}
12mg of mg^{2+}
9 mg of Al^{3+}

- PAR = Quantum sensor.

- AB – DTPA
↳ 1 M.

- Wheat straw : 80 : 1

- Decomposition – OM – Initially – Bacteria
Latest stages – Acti

- Radiation during night: Pyrheliometer
- EC = 1 dS/m = soluble salts ≈ 640 mg/L
- Urea: Highly hygroscopic.
- Clay: >35%

dimiv
dimis
0.034

Gypsum factor = 1.25.

- In analysis of variance – minn Df = 12
- Liming factor : 1.5–2.0.
- Dehydrogenase : C metabolism.
- Radius ratio of NH_4^+/K^+ is = 0.95 ~~0.143~~ / ~~0.133~~ 143/133
- Least equivalent acidity : NH_4NO_3.
- Three ~~error~~ errors : – strip plot.
- low phosphate potential : High avail of P.
- clostridium pasteurinum : Winogradsky.
- Rhizosphere :– Gram –ve spore
- soil consisting : Red & Black.
- First soil testing programme – 1955-56.
- Father of Natural Farming : Masanobu Fukuoka
- ATP $\xrightarrow{16\ kcal}$ ADP.
- National Bureau of Agri. Imp M/O – Mau Nath Bhajan, UP
- ~~Fool~~ $i = \frac{1}{2}t^{-\frac{1}{2}}$
- Radioactivity is a <u>First</u> order
- N— N_2 fixation by Legume → New Zealand.
- soil aeration limits — when H_2O filled pores > 50–60%.
- N-fixation → $N_2 \rightarrow NH_3$ → 8 e^-
- Normal soil C:N ratio :— 10:1
- Black colour of Black cotton soils — Titaneferous – clay humus.
- Calicoles prefer NO_3^-
- Na – flame photometer — Yellow colour.
- Karl Fischer' reagent — Iodine, SO_2, Pyridine
- Amphoteric : ~~Both 'a' & 'b'.~~ H_2O and alcohol

- Adsorption Isotherm – Low P conc.
- ~~Unif~~ degree of uniformity of distribution of data – Skewness.
- flatness / peakeness – kurtosis.

- Negative adsorp – repulsion
- Azotobacter – cereals.
- Maize indicator – P.
- Cl – pH not effect.
- Gypsum blocks – Reading Resistant – 400 – 600 ohms – FC.
- 1 ml of 1 N $K_2Cr_2O_7$ → 0.003 g C.
- AICRP (soil test crop response) – ISSS, Bhopal – – 1967
- 1 ml of 0.02 N H_2SO_4 = 0.00028 g of N.
- P use eff = 15 – 20 %
- Mango – tissue testing – Leaf + Petiole.
- Particular wavelength → absorbivity = emissivity (Kirchoff's law)

→ ↑Ca → ↓B
→ moderately mobile – Zn (plant)
→ Same formula → diff arrangement of atoms & prop ↳ Isomers

- Semi arid – arid → Columnar.
→ fixed on same site with P → Mo.
- Subsurface high density – brittle – Fragipan.
→ NO_3^- prodn – biologically driven – Warrington.
- subsurface of B horizon – Blocky.
→ H_2SO_4 → 18 M/36 N.

- p^H of calcareous soil in equilm with atm. CO_2 = 8.5
= Pressure of 1 atm = 76 cm vertical H_2O column or hydraulic head
- Black cotton soil or clayey = Blocky.
- OD = 2 − log T
- Not a specific pedogenic process :- Calcification.
- Maxm permissible limit of Biuret in urea → 1.5%.
- Lignin theory of humus :— Waksman.
- Change crystal shape with temp → NH_4NO_3.
- Francolite — $Ca_{10}(PO_4)_6 CO_3$
- ↓ value of Lime potential :— BC → more → more Lime.
- Major component in SSP → Gypsum.
- Ass. with fertilization and seed setting : Boron.
- °K + 273.15 = 87 °C $\frac{C}{5} = \frac{F-32}{9} = \frac{K-273}{5}$

  NH_4Cl — 128

  −30° = 243 / 30 ⇒ 8.
- Equi. acidity of NH_4NO_3 → 60.
- $CaCO_3$ equivalent of $MgCO_3$ is 119. - dolomite 109
- Equivalent basicity of $NaNO_3$ = 29.
  ↳ Na content = 27%.
- Per ha consumption of $N + P_2O_5 + K_2O$ India = 147 kg/ha.
= Equi. wt of $K_2Cr_2O_7$ in acidic medium = $\frac{1}{6}$th of mol. wt.
- Mandate crops of CIMMYT, Mexico — Wheat & Maize.
- Salt aff. in India : 10.4 Mha.
- IUSS situated at Aberdeen.
- Avg rainfall India = 1120 mm.
- In mineral soils - Mo ass. with — Amorphous R-oxide

64A

Fingerprint of IR region! – 800 – 1300 cm^{-1}.

– ASN : 0N

– P (Blue colour) – ascorbic a → Reducing a

– Wheat – salt loving.

– Ruinen – Phyllosphere.

MT^{-1}

– Surface tension – N/m

– size Ionic radii

I > Br > Cl > F

⇒ Gypsum equiva – elemental S = 0.18

– Irrigation when root zone moisture ↓ 10%.

– Radioactivity : Becquerel

excessive Mo – Cu deficiency

– Mo content in forage > 5 ppm – molybdenosis

– Of pH 5.0 and 6.0 mixed – equal quant
↳ result – 5.5

– Phenolpth – acid – colourless.

– FCO, 1985 – minm water soluble P_2O_5 – 41% in DAP

– Soil – mobility : N > K > P.

– Unit change pH = Eh 59.1 mV

– ↑ zeta potential – ↓ viscosity

– Zircon – lowest weatherability.

– KCl – neutral fert.

– Diff – coeff – 0.6 – 0.8

- Trees grow because of H_2O – Helmont
- Gobar gas - First – Germany.
- B regulates K/Ca ratio in plants
- avg P concn in soil soln → 0.5 ppm.
- Form Si – absorb – plant → $Si(OH)_4$.
- SSP – ↓volatiles - loss in compost
- ~~K~~ Salt Index – measure ↑ osmotic pressure of soil soln.
- IRSIC = Waginein.
- Mosaic map — physical & cultural features: – ~~Photomap~~ Soil Map.
- Food and Agricultural Org. of UN. developed a supra-national classification - also called World Soil Classfn → 26 soil classes.
- Waterlogged: Post hole auger.
- Histosol - negligible area in India.
- Peneplain → High area become→ Low area – due to erosion
- O horizon; OM > 20%.
- Ni containing. – Serpentine.
- A soil group of interzonal order and hydromorphic suborder consisting of soils with eleaviated surface horizon = Planosols.
- Solubility of gases in H_2O → Henry's Law.
- Uptake of P – problematic in waterlogged.
- Phreatophyte - ~~pr~~ ~~pd~~ subsurface H_2O.
- pH of blood – 7.3 – 7.4
- Vertical section of soil profile – mounted for display – Soil monolith
- Phosphogypsum → Cd as impurity.
- Wood ash – K_2CO_3

→ K in KCl → 50%

→ ~~-ve →~~ neutral atoms + e⁻ → -ve.

→ Father of soil micro. – Winogradsky

→ Y index – Martin & Russel.

– Microbial Transformation of N & S = Winogradsky.

pH < 5 – legumes not developed.

– E horizon – rare in grassland.

– Fungi – more in Rhizosphere.

– Azotobacter – Beijerinck.

– Nitrifying bac = – ve. Gram.

– specific heat of OM = 0.44.

– mulched soil – uniform heat flow.

– non capillary pores – > 15 μ.

–

- NITROGEN -

- ammonium ions - and some of the carbohydrates synthesized in leaves - converted into amino a̅ - mainly in green leaf itself.
- ↑ supply of nitrogen → ↑ rapid - the synthesized carbohy. converted into proteins and to protoplasm - smaller amount left available for cell wall material - which is mainly nitrogen free carbohydrates such as Ca pectate, cellulosans, cellulose and low nitrogen lignins.

Mass Spectometry

- analytical technique – ionizes chemical species and sorts the ions based on their mass to charge ratio.
- mass spectrum: plot of the ion signal as a function of mass to charge ratio. – used to determine the elemental/isotopic signature of a sample, the masses of particles and of molecules and to elucidate chemical structures of molecules.

- History

Modern techniques of mass spectroscopy – devised by Arthur Jeffrey Dempster and F.W Aston in 1918 and 1919 resp.

- Principle

- atoms or mol. – deflected by magnetic fields – provided they turn into an ion.
- electrically charged particles are affected by a magnetic field although electrically neutral ones aren't.

Sequence:–

i) Ionisation

- atom/mol ⟶ ionised – by knocking one or more electrons off to give a +ve ion — true even for those which we normally expect to form -ve ions (eg. Cl) or never forms ions at all (eg. Ar).
- Most mass spec. works with +ve ions.

ii) Acceleration

- ions – accelerated – so that they all have same kinetic energy.

iii) Deflection

- ions – deflected by a magnetic field acc. to their masses. —
- ↑ Lighter — more deflected.
- amount of deflection also depends on the no. of +ve charges on ion – ↑ ionised ⟶ more deflected.

iv) Detection

- beam of ions passing through the machine – detected electrically

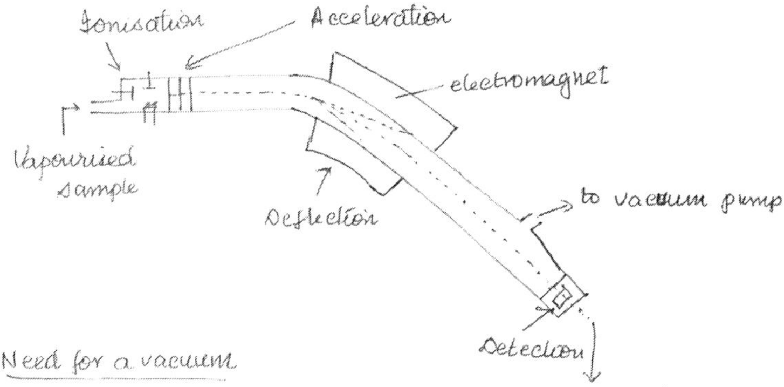

- Need for a vacuum
  - imp. that ions - in ionisation chamber have a free run through the machine without hitting air molecules.

Ionisation

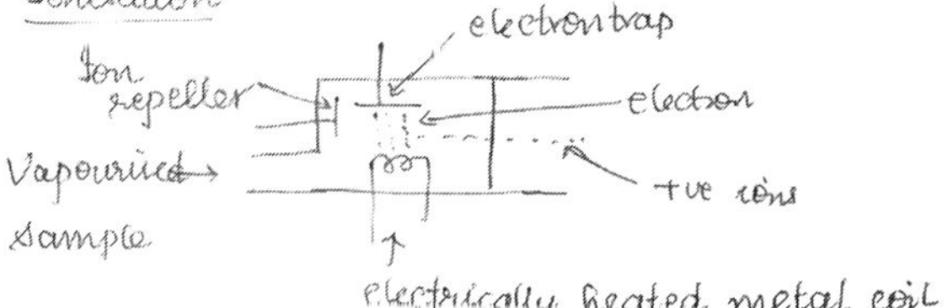

- vaporised sample ⟶ ionisation chamber —
- electrically heated coil — gives off e⁻ which are attracted to electron trap which is a +ve charged plate.
- particles in sample (atoms / mol.) — bombarded with stream of e⁻ and some of the collisions - energetic enough to knock one or more e⁻ out of sample particles ⟶ to give +ions.
- +ve ions - persuaded ~~out into the rest~~ by ion repeller (metal plate carrying a slight +ve charge)
- Ionisation chamber ⟶ +ve voltage of about 10,000 volts.

Acceleration

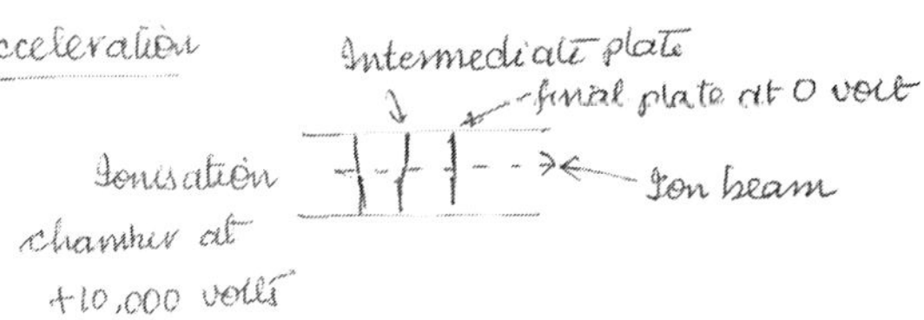

→ +ve ions – repelled away from the very +ve ionisation chamber – then pass – three slits – final one – 0 volt.

– middle slit – intermediate voltage.

– all ions – accelerated into a finely focused beam.

Deflection

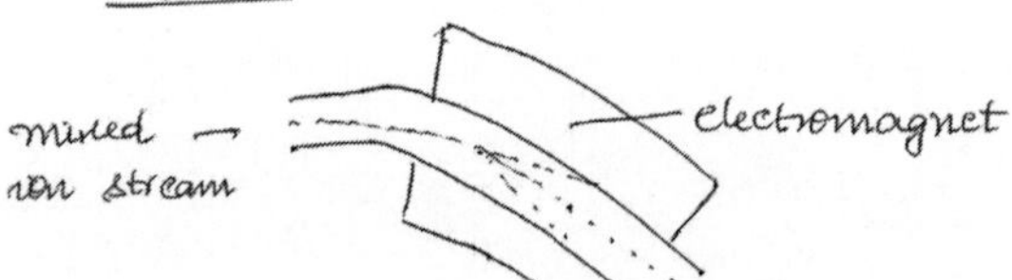

– diff ions deflected by magnetic field by diff amounts.

– amt. of deflection depends on:–

a) mass of an ion – lighter – deflected more.

b) charge ~~of~~ on an ion – Ions with 2 or > +ve charges – deflected more.

→ mass/charge ratio given by m/z

Detection

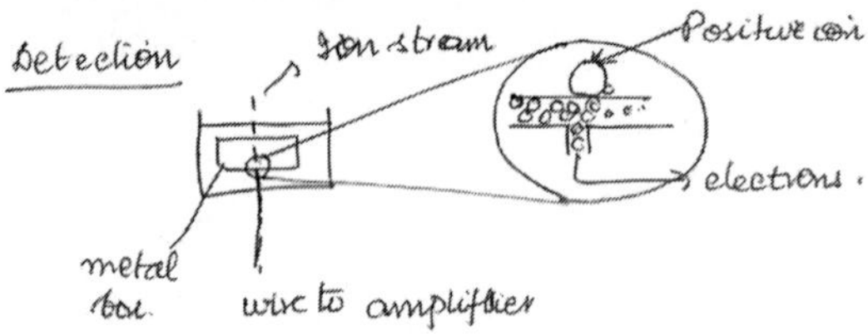

– only ion stream that make it right through the machine – ion detector.

– other ions collide with walls where they pick up e⁻ and be neutralised – eventually removed by vacuum pump.

– when ion hits metal box – charge neutralised by an e⁻ jumping from the metal on to the ion. That ~~leaves a space~~

~~Advantages~~

Colloids

- Colloidal chemistry of Inorganic soil constituents

- colloidal clay - < 2 μm
- Six soil silicates - based on the arrangement of SiO_4 tetrahedra in their structure:-

a) Cyclosilicates - closed rings or double rings of tetrahedra (SiO_3, Si_2O_5)

eg. Tourmaline, Benitoite.

b) Inosilicates - single or double chains of tetrahedra (SiO_3, Si_4O_{11})

eg. Pyroxene, amphibole, hornblende.

c) Nesosilicate - seperate SiO_4 tetrahedra.

eg. Olivine, garnet, zircon, topaz.

d.) Phyllosilicate - sheets of tetrahedra. (Si_2O_5)

eg. Vermiculite, kaolinite, smectite

e) Sorosilicate - two or more linked tetrahedra (Si_2O_7, Si_5O_{16})

eg. epidote

Refer ISSS classification

f) Tecto - framework (SiO_2)

eg. Feldspar, quartz, zeolite

- simplest - nesosilicate followed by soro. → cyclo - phyllo - tecto
- Amorphous soil colloids — silica ~~and~~ alumina, Fe oxides.
  - ↳ non-crystalline / paracrystalline clays.
  - ↳ short ~~order~~ range order (SRO) minerals
  - ↳ formed by rapid pedogenic process.
  - ↳ unstable
  - ↳ eventually crystallize in time → Long range order

Structural Chemistry of Clay Minerals

- Unit cell :- spatial arrangement of atoms producing unit cell → Lattice structure
  building unit of a crystal — unit layer
- Unit Lattice structure :- crystal arrangement - by placing several unit cells together.
- d spacings :- ~~interlayer~~ interplanar spacings.
- Basal (001) spacing — fundamental role in identification of clay minerals species by X-ray diffraction analysis.
- Miller indices — WH Miller — originally used symbols h, k, l for intercepts.

Structure of silicate clay

✓ Silicates - built around a Si tetrahedron — each O atom receives one valency from silicon atom.

✓ To satisfy its divalent requirement, O atom can be linked to other cations or to a neighbouring silicon atom of an adjacent silica tetrahedron.

✓ Linkage of silica tetrahedra — yields 5 groups of structural arrangements of silicate

✓ Silicate clay minerals — characterized by sheet structure

✓ stacked layers of silica tetrahedra and Al/Mg octahedral sheets

- ~~sheets~~ silica tetrahedra — arranged in hexagonal rings — sheets can indefinitely extend in a 2 dimensional direction acc. to planes a and b.
- ~~Com~~ In a network of Si tetrahedra — One oxygen in each tetrahedron — remains electrically unbalanced — satisfy the divalent requirement by linking to Al in octahedral co-ordination.

- Unit structure: - total assembly of a layer plus interlayer material -
- On the basis of the no. of tetrahedral to octahedral sheets in one layer -
  - 1:1 — dimorphic
  - 2:1 — trimorphic
  - 2:2/2:1:1 — tetramorphic
  - 2:2 → chlorite; 2:1:1 ↳ Palygorskite and sepiolite
- each clay mineral group < dioctahedral / trioctahedral subgroups.
- If two of three octahedral positions — occupied by Al^{3+} — dioctahedral.
- If all octahedral positions are occupied by Mg^{2+} — trioctahe.
- Interstratified group of clay minerals — two or more diff. types of unit layers — stacked together.

Kaolinite

- hydrated aluminosilicate — general chemical composition of $Al_2O_3 : SiO_2 : H_2O = 1:2:2$ or $2SiO_2 \cdot Al_2O_3 \cdot 2H_2O$ per unit cell.
  White (2005) — $Si_2O_5Al_2(OH)_4$.
- 1:1 phyllosilicates
- aluminum oct. sheets stacked above Si tetra. sheets.
- sheets extend continuously in a and b direction and — stacked one above another in z or c direction. - unit cell — non symmetrical - si tet. on one side and Al oct. on another
- Basal plane of O atoms in one crystal unit — opposite basal plane of another composed of OH ions of next layer.
- 2 sheets ~~held~~ forming a unit layer — held together by O atoms — mutually shared by Si and Al atoms in respective sheets.
- So, unit layers, in turn, held together by hydrogen bonding.
- Basal spacing (001) of kaolinite — 7.14 Å.
- little isomorphous substitution — permanent charge per unit cell. - if not zero - very small.

- owing to presence of exposed OH groups — variable or pH dependent, –ve charge.
  - dissociates into H^+.
- Cation exc. capacity is very small
- Because of tightness of structural bonds — plasticity and shrinkage and swelling prop.
- sp. surface area – 7 – 30 m^2/g.
- thickness – 0.05 – 2 μm. – hexagonal form.
- Presence of kaolinite – identified by a (001)d spacing of 7.14 Å X ray diffraction and a 2nd order 3.57 Å diffraction in oriented samples. – Diffraction peaks – disappear after kaolinite – 500 – 550°c.
- Members: kaolinite, dickite, nacrite and halloysite
  - halloysite upon heating — irreversibly dehydrated — then called metahalloysite
- kaolinite – most widely distributed in soil out of 1:1 mineral
- Imp. fraction of ultisols and oxisols.
- accessory minerals – alfisols and vertisols in tropics.

Halloysite

- general composition $Al_2O_3 : SiO_2 : H_2O = 1:2:4$.
- structure similar to kaolinite
- differences: – disordered stacking of layers and in the presence of two or more interlayers of H_2O
  - H_2O molecules linked together in a hexagonal pattern.
  - bonded to crystal structure by
- Hydrogen bonding
- Because of presence of H_2O molecules – (001)d spacing = 10.1 Å, → which upon heating reduces to 7.2 Å.

- dehydrated sp = meta halloysite
- Halloysite $\xrightarrow[\text{rapid}]{50°C}$ metahalloysite
  ↳ but basal d spacing - collapse only at 400°c.
  ↓
- but heating doesn't affect random stacking of layers.
- Tubular form - electron microscopy — considered to be a rolled-up sheet
- ↳ Because of presence of interlayer H_2O — normal to axis
  bonding of O-OH groups — prevented — causing a distortion of crystal structure with the consequent curling of layers.
- X-ray diffraction pattern of halloysite — 10.5 Å — almost similar to kaolinite.
- Formation and stability → influenced by soil moisture.
- moist → reqd. for development.
- Indications that halloysite - precursor of kaolinite.
  Igneous rock → smectite → halloysite → metahalloysite → kaolinite.

Smectite

General formula
Ratio
Bonding
Basal
charge
Planes

- variable composition
- $Al_2O_3 \cdot 4SiO_2 \cdot H_2O + xH_2O$.
- white (2005) —

$$[(OH)_2(Si_{3.74}Al_{0.26})(Al_{1.77}Mg_{0.23})O_{10}]^{-0.49} \; 0.49M^+.$$

M^+ — Interlayer cation — neutralizing -ve charge of mineral

- Principal end members in dioctah. subgroup :—
  - beidellite — high Al content — Si layer charge through isomo. sub. of Al^{3+} for Si^{4+}.
  - nontronite — all Al^{3+} replaced by Fe^{3+}.
- Mg or Fe^{3+} ions in octahedral sheet.

- Trioctahedral :—
  - hectorite - fibrous
  - saponite

Plasticity
swelling & Shr.
sp. surf area
CEC
Thickness
Shape

Identification
Members.
Imp fraction.

FRIB BCPP SSS
CIMT.

- Two hypothesis – on structure < Hofmann and Endele; Edelman and Favajee }

- Both hypothesis – similar – unit cell structure is symmetrical unlike kaolinite.

- One Al oct. sheet – sandwiched between 2 Si tet. sheets.
- bonds holding layers – relatively weak – so. develop intermicellar spaces – expand with ↑ moisture content.
- Diff in hypothesis – arrangement of Si tetr. network.
- Edelman and Favajee – alternative arrang. of Si tetrahedra with Si-O-Si bond angle = 180° with – basal planes composed of OH groups bonded by Si in the tetrahedrons.

- Hofman and Endele – Si-O. – alternating.

- –ve charge – isom. subst.
- Only small variable charge – as all disposable hydroxyl groups located in subsurface planes covered by a network of O atoms.

- sp. surface area – 700–800 m²/g – exposed on dispersion in H_2O.
- High swell-shrink capacity – increase in basal spacing – form occuring stepwise – formation of hydration shells around interlayer cations – a for metal ions and organic compounds.

- Adsorption of org. compounds (glycerol and ethylene glycol) – used as a +ve/diagnostic identification of smectite by XRD analysis.
- Oven dry (105°C) – characterized basal spacing of 10 Å.
- Air dry – 12.4 to 14 Å
- After solvation or intercalation with ethylene glycol or glycerol – 17 Å.
- Among several sp. of clays – smectite – most widely distributed.
- Most soil smectites (montm) are dioctahedral.

- Charact. constituents of Vertisols, Mollisols and Alfisols.

Illites
(non expanding 2:1 clays)

- micaceous clay
- In contrast with true micas (primary) ⟶ illite – secondary minerals.
- hydrous mica.
- finer grained minerals – illite.
  coarser ———— hydrous mica.
- almost similar chemical composition like muscovite – but contains more SiO_2 and less K.
- Contrast to mica – Illite – exhibits some isom. sub. of Al^{3+} for Si^{4+} in tetrahedral sheets and some subs. of Al^{3+} for Mg and Fe in octahedral sheet.
- White (2005)

$$[(OH)_2(Si_{3.3}Al_{0.7})(Al_{1.33}Mg_{0.4}Fe_{0.3})O_{10}]^{-1.3}\ 1.3K^{+}$$

- Primarily K – but sometimes NH_4^+ – occupy trigonal cavities formed by adjacent siloxal surfaces.
- Illite between smectite and muscovite.

$$H_2KAl_3Si_3O_{12} \xleftrightarrow[\text{Illite series}]{} 6Al_2O_3.4SiO_2.H_2O + xH_2O.$$

- Because illite contains K in interlayer — bonded unit layers – more strongly than smectite.
- Because of electrostatic bonds exerted by K^+ ions – (001) spacing is 10 Å.
- Charac. XRD — basal spacing of 10 Å
  ↓
  Peak doesn't shift or even collapse after heating the mineral at 500°C or after solvation with glycerol or ethylene glycol.
- Another diagnosis: — elemental analysis of K conc.

- Theoretical concn – 9-10% K. But frequent – 5-8%. with avg. 7%.
- Mollisol, Alfisol. Spodosol, Aridisol, Inceptisol, Entisol.
- In areas – heavy ppt – altered into smectite
- In warmer areas / high temp – structure of illite – disordered – form kaolinite

Vermiculite

- also forms mica-like flakes like illites
- also a mica alteration product
- Two categories – true vermiculite → rock forming mineral. / clay " → clay-sized.

hydrobiotite – not vermiculite – but it is illite group (from weathering of biotite)

because upon heating – Becomes elongated, twisted and curled. – expands 20-30 times of original size.

(derived from vermiculare or ← vermicularis – Latin word 'wormlike' or 'to breed worms'.

- Often called 14 A° mineral because – detection in soils based on XRD peak at 14 Å. – Peak won't shift / collapse upon solvation. But after 700°c – basal – 11.8 or 9.3 Å.
- Clay-verm – magnesium aluminium silicate – Mg occupy octa. positions between 2 Si tetr. sheets

- $Mg_3Si_4O_{10}(OH)_2 \times H_2O$
- structure similar to chlorite ~~but diff~~ – instead of brucite – H_2O mol. of about 5 A° layers – occupy intermicellar spaces.
- In some cases – interlayering with hydroxy-Al also occurs.
- In tetrahedral layer – considerable substitution of Al for Si takes place. – reason for high -ve charge present in vermi.
- largest CEC among inorg. colloids.
- CEC of dioctah. vermi = 1.05 times of trioctah.

- Presence of hydroxy Al interlayers – usually reduces CEC of mineral —— called hydroxyaluminium interlayer vermiculite (HIV) – also called interstratified verm.
  - → low CEC.

- most verm – dioctahedral.
- have wedge zones with ↑ selectivity for fixation of K^+, NH_4^+ and other cations.
- accessory minerals in clay fraction of Ultisols, Mollisols and Aridisols.
- formed more in well drained soils whereas smectite requires gley condition.

Chlorite

- hydrated Mg and Al silicates – related to mica minerals in appearance.
- name comes from its green colour.
- Octahedral sheets – composed of $Mg(OH)_2$ (called brucite sheet) – sandwiched between 2 silica tetrahedral sheets
- Intermicellar spaces occupied by brucite. so 2:2 clays.
- variable in composition – however, general

$$(Mg, Fe, Al)_6 (Si, Al)_4 O_{10} (OH)_8$$

- Isom. sub can occur in both tetra. and octa. layers.
- Si – replaced by Al.
- Fe or Al may replace Mg

} – degree of substitution expressed by Foster (1962) as Fe^{2+}/R^{2+} ratios.

a) Fe chlorites – containing ↑ relatively amts of Fe^{2+} (↑ $\frac{Fe^{2+}}{R^{2+}}$ rat) → called chamosite

b) Intermediates

c) Mg chlorites – smaller Fe (↓ Fe^{2+}/R^{2+} ratio)
   → clinochlore

- replacement of Mg by Al – in brucite – develops +ve charge –

(practically neutralizes –ve charge of mica layer

↳ so chlorite small –ve charge.

and small CEC.

- hydroxy interlayers – sites for anion retention eg. P.

but reduces K^+, NH_4^+ fixation.

- Basal → 14 A° – doesn't shift upto 500°C.
- Swelling chlorite – 28 A° → 32°A by solvation.
- Abundance low.
- accessory – Alfisol, Mollisol.
- most chlorite trioctahedral.

Surface chemistry of soil clays

- Three surfaces :-
  - a) formed mainly by Si-O-Si linkages of silica tetrahedron
  - b) " " " O-Al-OH " " alumina octa.
  - c) " " " Al-OH, Si-OH and Fe-OH of amorphous compounds.

a) surface planes of O atoms underlaid by Si atoms of the tetrahedrons.
- Si-O-Si bond - siloxane bond - Stikher and Bach (1966)
- ↳ plane of O atoms - siloxane surface - typical of 2:1 clay

divided: Innersphere / Outersphere

- Si tetrahedrons - arranged in hexagonal rings - hexagonal cavities developed in siloxane surface - 2.6 Å diameter.
- surface in siloxane cavity - Inner sphere surface
- those of exposed site of siloxane surface - outer.
- Size of H_2O - 3 Å - so - H_2O - not able to penetrate cavity - otherwise would dissolve and decompose clays.
- so, complexing H_2O by innersphere surf - not possible but adsorption of cations - feasible - smaller sizes.

b) planes of exposed hydroxyl, OH, groups underlaid by Al, Fe or Mg atoms in the center of octahedrons. - oxyhydroxy surface.
- 1:1 clay - siloxane surface on basal plane and oxyhydroxy surface on other basal plane.
- exposed OH ⟶ dissociates - so develop -ve charge.

c) - Si-OH - silonal surfaces
- Al-OH - aluminol surfaces
- Fe-OH - ferrol "

} - present in soils cont. large amts of silica gel, amorp. Al and Fe oxides, allophane.

- Broken edge of octahedral sheet - OH groups - coordinated to Al in the octahedron.
- Broken edge of tetra. - OH groups - OH - Si.

- Silanol-OH – capable of dissociating its proton due to larger valence of Si.
- aluminol-OH — dissociate its proton as well as adsorb an extra proton.

Dissociation → produces -ve charge on broken edge.
↓
neutralize +ve charge created by protonation of aluminol-OH or may increase -ve charge in the event of dissociation of aluminol-OH.

Surface areas

Total surface area = $A = \frac{\pi L^3}{d}$ square units.

L = width
d = diameter.

- specific surf area
  = $\frac{\text{surface area}}{\text{unit volume or mass of particles}}$

  = $\frac{6}{d}$ square units/cubic unit.
  eg. mm^2/mm^3.

- SSA for clay minerals by 3 diff. methods. (CPB = cetyl pyridinium bromide)

	H_2O method m^2/g	CPB	N_2 Gas
Smectite	300	800	784
Mica-smectite (interstratified)	57	152	109
Kaolinite	17	15	32
Allophane	484	0	157

- moodd ~~modd~~	– goodd ~~godd~~	– tigon
- sit	– lisen	– ladaq
- Lit	– las	– men
- regur	– 0	– lust

Origin of -ve charges in soil clays

i) Isomorphous subs.

- major source in 2:1 clays.
- Sposito (1989, 2008) – permanent structural charge, σ_p (measure through)

$$\sigma_p = -\left(\frac{X}{M_r}\right)$$

X — layer charge/unit formula; M_r — relative molecular mass.

eg. $\sigma_p = \frac{-0.50}{719}$ for smectite/montmor.

$= -0.0006954$ Eq/g $\times 10^6$

$= -69.5$ mEq/100 g

$= -69.5$ cmol/kg

$= -0.695$ mol/kg.

- The ease which IS takes place depends on –
  a) size – comparable size – < 15%.
  b) valence of ions involved. – should not differ more than one unit

ii) Dissociation of exposed hydroxyl groups.

- Mehlich (1981) prefer the term 'pH dependent charge' over 'variable charge'.
  - Sposito (1989) – quantitative interpretation in terms of proton charge σ_H

$$\sigma_H = m_H - m_{OH}$$

m_H — mol/L of H^+ ions; m_{OH} — mol/L of OH^- ions complexed by surface functional groups.

- Intrinsic surface charge. σ_i = sum of $\sigma_p + \sigma_H$

$$\sigma_i = \sigma_p + \sigma_H$$

when $\sigma_H > \sigma_p$ → soil has variable charge –

- ~~Not only can protons be dissociated from~~ expo

Positive charges and ZPC

- soil colloids - Both -ve and +ve charges
  ↓ make possible anion exchange reactions - phosphate retention.
  ↙ arise from protonation or addition of H^+ ions to hydroxyl groups.
  ↓ more imp. in Al and Fe oxide clays - less imp in Si-oxides.
  e.g. Gibbsite is +vely charged at pH 7 or lower.

- ZPC → pH_0
- pH values above pH_0 → colloid -ve charged
- pH values below pH_0 → " +ve charged.

- Three types of ZPCs (Sposito, 1989)
  - ↳ ZPC → $\sigma_p + \sigma_H = 0$
  - ↳ ZPPC — Zero point proton charge where $\sigma_H = 0$ and
  - ↳ ZPNC — Zero point net charge where

$$\sigma_e + \sigma_{os} + \sigma_{is} = 0$$

effective surface charge influenced by DDL ions

surface charge of outersphere

surf. ch. of inner.

↓ as represent total surface plane of clay

↓ sum of outer + inner charges = Intrinsic surf. charge

$$\sigma_{i} = \sigma_{os} + \sigma_{is}$$

So,

$$\sigma_p + \sigma_H = \sigma_{os} + \sigma_{is} \ (= 0 \text{ at ZPNC})$$

- At ZPNC → surface mineral – 0 charge and not be able to attract a diffuse layer of counter ions. – so σ_e obsolete

- Determine ZPC – by titration method or by analysis of amts of adsorbed cations and anions as a function of pH and concen.

↳ of H^+ and OH^- ions – main potential determining ions –
ZPC found out by potentiometric titration

$$\sigma = F(\Gamma_{H^+} - \Gamma_{OH^-})$$

σ – Surface charge density; F – Faraday's constant; Γ_{H^+}, Γ_{OH^-} – adsorption densities of H^+ and OH^- → meq/g.

- Use of ΔpH – in determination of –ve or +ve charge or 0. →

analyses of soil pH in 1 N KCl and in water.

$$\Delta pH = pH_{H_2O} - pH_{KCl}.$$

↳ +ve = presence of –vely charged clay colloid.
→ ZPC is reached when ΔpH = 0.
–ve = +vely charged.

Surface potential

Surface pot ψ, Nernst eqn

$$\psi = \left[\frac{RT}{nF}\right] \cdot \ln \frac{(H^+)}{(H^+)_{ZPC}}$$

$$= 0.059\,[\log (H^+) - \log (H^+)_{ZPC}]$$

$$= 0.059\,(ZPC - pH) \text{ volts at } 25^\circ C.$$

Difference between ZPC and Isoelectric Point

(a) (1)
- p^H at which surface exhibits a neutral net electrical charge = ZPC at surface.

- Isoelectric :— value of p^H at which colloidal particles remains stationary in an electric field.

- ZPC = Iso — when no specific adsorption on surface.

J.P
- Jolivet (2000) — in absence of +ve/−ve charges — surface is

(b) best described by ZPC.

- If +ve and −ve charges are both present in equal amounts — isoelectric point.

(3) ZPC = absence of any type of surface charge

- IEP = state of neutral net charge.

- Diff - quantity of charged sites at point of net 0 charge.

- Jolivet - uses intrinsic surface equil^m constants pK^- and

(4) pK^+ to define these two conditions in terms of relative no. of charged sites.

$$pK^- - pK^+ = \Delta pK = \log \frac{[MO:}{[MOH_2^+]}$$

- If large ΔpK (>4 acc. to Jolivet) — predominant ~~sp~~ species is MOH — while there are relatively few charged sp → ZPC.

- For small values ΔpK, there are many charged sp in approx. equal amts — IEP

Soil colloids

Properties of soil colloids

(I) - colloids - heterogeneous mixture - 2 phases < dispersion medium / dispersed phase.

(II) - true size of soil colloids - < 2 μm.

Ionic solution ← 2nm - 200 nm → suspension

Some schools of thoughts

uni phase solution ← 1μm - 1nm → suspension

(III) Colloidal solution - light scattered randomly - Tyndall scattering.

(IV) Brownian movement - due to unbalanced impact of solvent mol. on colloidal particles - these particles move in zig zag way in solution. Upper limit - 0.0002 mm.

(V) Sheet like morphology - so high aspect ratio, ↑ specific surface and charges.

(VI) Both lyophilic - because of their hydration tendency
lyophobic - because of their sensitivity towards electrolyte.

(VII) clay - humus - complex - most reactive component of soil - control bfn - buffering, filtering, nutrient supply.

(VIII) Soil colloids < Inorganic / Organic

- aluminosilicate layer lattice clay
- hydrous oxides & hydroxides of Fe, Al, Si, Mn.
- amorphous silicates.

↳ on the basis of
- nature of linkages present
- bo types of compounds formed

Inorganic soil colloids

Addition Gouy-chapman Diffuse layer

$\rightarrow K = 3 \times 10^7 z \pm \sqrt{c}$

value of $\frac{1}{K}$ is usually as a measure of thickness of double layer.

If c ↑ 4x → K ↑ with a factor of $\sqrt{4} = 2$.

So, thickness of double layer $(\frac{1}{K})$ ↓ $\frac{1}{2}x$ from surface.

Effect of electrolytes on thickness of DDL

- Chesworth (2005) – thickness – 1-10 nm.
- thickness ↓ as valence and conc of soln electrolytes ↑.
- suppression.
- ↑ concn → amount of cation ↑ → reduces concn gradient in liquid interface between colloidal surface and surrounding liquid phase. – tendency to diffuse ↓ – ↓ thickness.

Effect of valence of cations on thick. of DDL

- Monovalent > Divalent > Trivalent.

Limitations of Gouy Chapman DDL

- ~~develope~~ developed for application on flat surfaces – but may equally apply well to rounded or spherical surfaces.
- –ve charge evenly distributed over surface.
- counterions – assumed as point charges – occupy no spaces.
- takes into account simple electrostatic force – by which cations with similar valence are adsorbed similarly.

Zeta Potential (ζ)

- When colloidal suspension placed - electrical field - collo. part. move in one direction (towards +ve pole). Countenions move in another direction (towards -ve pole)
- electric pot. developed at solid - liquid interface.
- seat of ζ potential — shearing plane/slipping plane between bulk liquid an an envelope of H_2O moving with the particle.
- As position of shearing plane - unknown — zeta pot — represents elec. pot. at an unknown distance from colloidal surf.

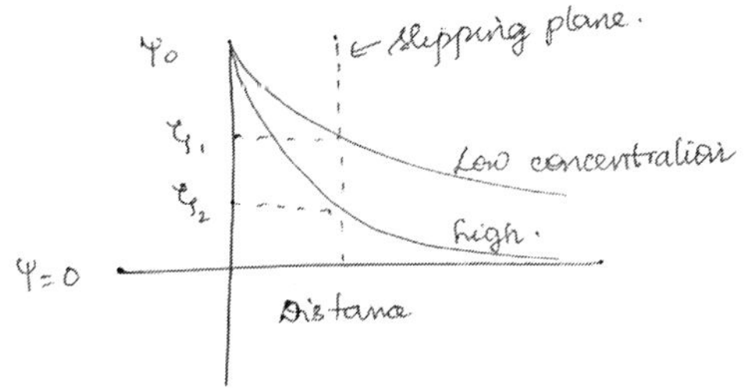

- effect of electrolytes
  - ↑ electro. concn → solution → ↓ DDL.
  - Reaches a critical value (→ elec. concn) — at which ζ potential = 0 = Isoelectric point — DDL very thin — particle repulsive forces are at a minimum.
    → At and below this point → repulsion — not longer strong — so flocculation
- ζ pot. — not a unique prop. of colloid - but depends on surface pot (Ψ) of clay.
- Determined by electrophoretic mobility of suspension.

$$V_e = \frac{(D\zeta E)}{4\pi\eta} = \frac{D\zeta E}{4\pi\eta}$$

D = diele. constant
E = applied emf
η = visco. of fluid.

V_e → electrokinetic velocity

- ζ pot – electrokinetic pot at slipping plane surf.
- surface pot – Ψ_0 – dilute solution – electrok. pot. – has a value represented by ζ_1 – when salt added – diffuse layer suppressed – more counterions forced to colloid surface within the slipping plane
  ↓ at fixed distance.
  so, at ↑ salt concⁿ – change occurs in total pot. distribution as related to distance from colloid.
- so, ζ_2 is smaller than ζ_1.

Adsorption

Types (a)

↳ positive: – concⁿ of solute on colloidal surface $pH \leq 4$
 – also known as specific adsorption
 – solute usually decreases surface tension.

↳ negative – concⁿ of solvent on clay surface. $pH > 4$.
 – solute – concentrated in bulk solution – till $pH = pKa$
 – surface tension ↑.

affected by soil pH and pKa of organic adsorbates.

–ve adsorption → dominant pH > 4
+ve adsorption → " " ≤ 4

– ve adsorp of org. ā → occurs first till pH in soil approaches pKa of adsorbate → after which +ve adsorp. takes places and ↑ as pH ↓.

Bailey and White (1970) – +ve adsorp – pH 1–1.5 pH higher than the disso. constant of org. ā

- Bailey and White – (1970) – surface acidity of adsorbent
↓
H^+ ion concn in interface.

- org. compounds → -vely adsorbed by Na smectite pH 6.8.
+vely adsorbed by H smectite pH 3.35

(b) specific and nonspecific.
- specific :– also called +ve adsorp, chemisorption (Schwertmann and Taylor 1977)

- non specific. – adsorption reaction related to electrostatic bonding of solutes by clay.

Sposito – complexation of solutes by outersphere surfaces of clay minerals.

White (2005) – caused by an attractive force over and above the simple electrostatic force.
- recognizes two groups of ions affected by it
a) monovalent : . Li < Na < K < Rb < Cs.
↳ form mostly innersphere complexes.
- smaller the size ∴ remains hydrated.
- whereas Cs – dehydrated at surface to strongly adsorbed.
- H_2O mol. in hydration shell of ion – polarized – initiating an adsorption process – was known as water bridging.

b) Divalent : Mg < Ca < Sr < Ba < Ra.
- form outersphere complexes because they retain upon adsorption. their hydration H_2O.

ADSORPTION ISOTHERMS

- Curve relating the concentrations of adsorbed materials at fixed temperature.
- Two methods — in use of ad. iso. to study ~~ad~~ behaviour of adsorption reactions.
    - a) identification of shape and ~~curvat~~ curvature of adsorp. isotherm.
    - b) statistical formulation — statistical modelling.

4 basic types.

- a) S type :- when solid — high affinity for solvent
- b) L-type :- solid — " " " solute

predict similar things as Langmuir adsorp. isotherm.

- c) C-type : — also known as constant partition isotherm.
    - constant partitioning of solute between solution and adsorbent.
    - common when new adsorption sites become available as solute is adsorbed from soln.
- d) H-type — also called high affinity curve.
    - solute — ↑ affinity for solid.
    - considered special type of L curve.
    - In dilute soln — solute completely adsorbed and no measurable amount — left in soln.

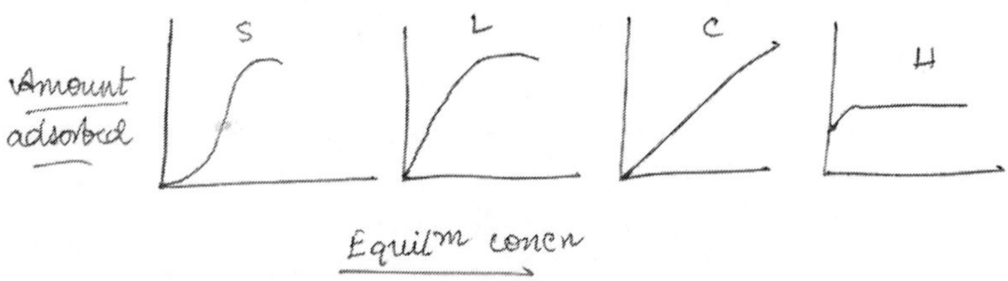

- Statistical modelling – Four major types of equations –
  - a) Freundlich (1926)
  - b) Langmuir (1918)
  - c) BET (1938)
  - d) Gibbs equation.

Freundlich equation

- originally formulated by ~~J.M~~ J.M van Van Bemmelen in 1888.
- popularized by Freundlich (1926)
- is, all in fairness – Van Bemmelen – Freundlich eqn.
- adsorp. isotherm in mainly dilute soln →

$\frac{x}{m} = kC^{1/n}$ — Freundlich exponent. $\frac{1}{n}$

- x – amt of mat adsorbed
- m – amt of adsorbent
- C – concn of equilm solution
- k – Freundlich adsorption constant

- no theoretical foundation – emperical in nature.
- value of $\frac{1}{n}$ ⇒ 0.2 – 0.7
  - For pesticides ⇒ $\frac{1}{n} = 1$
  - If $\frac{1}{n} = 1$ → eqn – linear eqn $\frac{x}{m} = kC$.
- curve – parabolic (exponential)
  - showing :– a) no single point indicating process is complete
  - b) no region of discontinuity

- Logarithm form

$$\log\left(\frac{x}{m}\right) = \log k + \frac{1}{n}\log C.$$

- log eqn gives a straight line or linear curve

BET AND GAB

- Stephen Brunauer, Paul Hugh Emmett and Edward Teller (1938)
  - adsorption of multilayers of non polar gases.
- Reversed by Brunauer, Deming, Deming and Teller in 1946.
- Bailey and White (1970) – BET used to describe 5 types of adsorption reactions :–
  - a) monolayer adsorption
  - b) sigmoid shape monolayer ads.
  - c) mono. ads. plus capillary condensation
  - d) multilayer ads.
  - e) " " plus capillary "
- Extension of BET model – developed by Guggenheim – Anderson – de Boer (GAB)

$$W = \frac{W_m C_g K\left(\frac{P}{P_0}\right)}{\left[1-K\left(\frac{P}{P_0}\right)\right]\left[1-K\left(\frac{P}{P_0}\right)+C_g K\left(\frac{P}{P_0}\right)\right]}$$

W_m – wt. in grams of a monolayer of adsorbed H_2O.

W – wt. in grams of adsorbed H_2O/g solid.

P – equil^m vapour press.

P_0 – saturation vp.

C_g, K – parameters related to heat of adsorption of monolayer and intermediate layer resp.

GIBBS

- processes in relation to surface tension

$$\Gamma = -\left(\frac{a}{RT}\right)\left(\frac{d\gamma}{da}\right)_T$$

Γ – surface concn of adsorbed material (moles/cm²)

a – activity of solute in moles

γ – surface tension dynes/cm.

R – gas constant

T – absolute temp.

- solute adsorbed on surface of adsorbent if $d\gamma/da = -ve$ ie $\Gamma = +ve$

  ↓

  positive adsorption → solute ↓ surface tension

If $\frac{d\gamma}{da}$ = +ve ie Γ = −ve ⇒ solute more concn in bulk soln — negative adsorp — solute ↑ Surf. tension.

- primary application in adsorption at liquid gas interface.
- but difficult at solid - liquid interface — as impossible to measure γ of solid surfaces

Cation exchange capacity

$CEC = S \times \sigma$ — surface charge density
S — specific surface

$$\sigma = \frac{\sqrt{2\varepsilon n k T}}{\pi \sinh (Ze\psi_0/2kT)}$$

Emperical equations of cation exchange

- I) Freundlich Equation $x = KC^{1/n}$ — express conc composition in soil solution
- II) Langmuir - Vageler equation — adaptable for narrow range of adsorption.

$\frac{x}{x^0} = \frac{KC}{1+KC}$

$x = \frac{(K_1 + CB)}{K_2 + C}$ = Langmuir - Vageler eqn.

B — Base exchange capacity of soils
C — initial concn of exchanger ion
x — amt of cations exchanged

Mass action law equations

- Kerr
- Vanselow
- Gapon

Kinetic eqns of cation exc

- Gapon (1933), Jenny (1936) and Davis (1945).
- Gaines and Thomas (1955) also develop — as reported by Krishnamoorthy and Overstreet, Jenny and Davies

Soil colloid — Ca + $2Na^+$ ⟶ Colloid − 2Na + Ca^{2+}.

$$\frac{[Na^+]^2 (Ca^{2+})}{[Ca^{2+}] (Na^+)^2} = K \, [Na^+ + Ca^{2+}]$$

Rearranging Gaines and Thomas model ↑ above :- gives.. →

$$\frac{[Na^+]^2 (Ca^{2+})}{\{[Ca^{2+}](Na^+)^2 [Na^+ + Ca^{2+}]\}} = K.$$

Thermodynamic eqns of cation exc

- Gaines and Thomas (1955)

For a general reaction involving monovalent cations A^+ and B^+ the equation at equilm

micelle − A + B^+ ⟷ micelle − B + A^+

Application of mass action law gives: —

$$K_{eq} = K_{ex} = \frac{[B^+] (A^+)}{[A^+] (B^+)}$$ ✓

Free energy change, ΔG_r

$$\Delta G_r = \Delta G_r^o + RT \ln \frac{[B^+](A^+)}{[A^+] (B^+)}$$ ✓

or $\Delta G_r = \Delta G_r^o + RT \ln K_{ex}$.

At equilm $\Delta G_r = 0$ then following eqn is valid

$$\Delta G_r = 0 = \Delta G_r^o + RT \ln K_{ex}$$

$$\Rightarrow \Delta G_r^o = -RT \ln K_{ex}$$

$$\Rightarrow \Delta G_r^o = -1.364 \log K_{ex} \text{ at } 25°C = 298 K.$$

↓

selectivity coefficient (known as activity coefficient) └ sparks (2003)

Quantity-Intensity (Q/I) Relation

- originally presented by Beckett (1964) for studying rate of exchange of K in soils by Ca, or by Ca & Mg
- Relative abundance and availability of free and exc. cations to plants in relation to the amt. of cations adsorbed by soil colloids.
- Quantity :— concn of K in soils – liberated by exchange with Ca.
- Intensity – activity ratio of free ions K/Ca or K/Ca+Mg

$$\frac{Q}{I} = \frac{a_K}{\sqrt{a_{(Ca+Mg)}}}$$ (activity)

By applying thermodynamic concepts —

$$RT \ln \frac{Q}{I} = \frac{a_K}{\sqrt{a_{Ca+Mg}}}$$

$$\Delta G^0_r = -RT \ln \frac{Q}{I}$$

$$= \frac{a_K}{\sqrt{a_{Ca+Mg}}}$$

- expressed in a curve — in which factor quantity represented by ΔK on Y axis, relating change in concn of K in soil soln.
— intensity factor – recorded in abscissa representing activity ratio.

$$\text{Activity ratio} = \frac{[(K^+)\gamma_K]}{(\sqrt{Ca^{2+}})(\gamma_{Ca})^{1/2}}$$

γ – activity coeff — calculated through Debye - Huckel formula.

$$AR^K = \frac{a_K}{\sqrt{a_{Ca^{2+}}}}$$

- Q/I curve – characteristic – as upper part linear whereas bottom part is curvilinear in regression.

- Linear part – special case of Gapon equation – attributed to non specific sites for K related to planar surfaces.
- Curvilinear portion – caused by specific sites with a high affinity for K.

- AR_e^K value or equil(m/e) activity ratio of K = measure of availability (intensity) of labile K in soils.

- AR_e^K ↑ — K fertilization.
  ↓ — liming

- Van Schouwenburg and Schuffelen (1963) —
  $AR_e^K < 0.001$ — K adsorbed on edge position
  > 0.001 — planar surfaces.

- Intersect of linear curve with Y axis – obtained by extrapolation is called ΔK^0 — which together with ΔK – represents exc. K or labile K pool.

$$[K] = \Delta K + \Delta K^0$$

↓

amt of K adsorbed on exch. sites

↓

- ↑ with K fertilization and liming

- ΔK^0 → more -ve ↑ lime / fertilization — indicating more K release – soil soln.
- When adsorp. K → on planar – value of ΔK^0 – compares favorbly to amount of K extracted by NH_4OAc method.
- When adsorp. mainly on specific sites — values ΔK^0 → smaller than extracted.

- slope of linear portion of the curve represented by $\frac{\Delta K}{\Delta AR^K} = PBC^K$ or potential buffering capacity for K. — related to CEC of soil — measure of soil's capacity to maintain concⁿ of K (intensity) at a constant value in soil.

- ↑ PBC^K → ↑ K availability
- ↓ PBC^K — need for K fertilization.
- PBC^K → ↑ → with lime addition — due to ↑ in pH dependent charges.

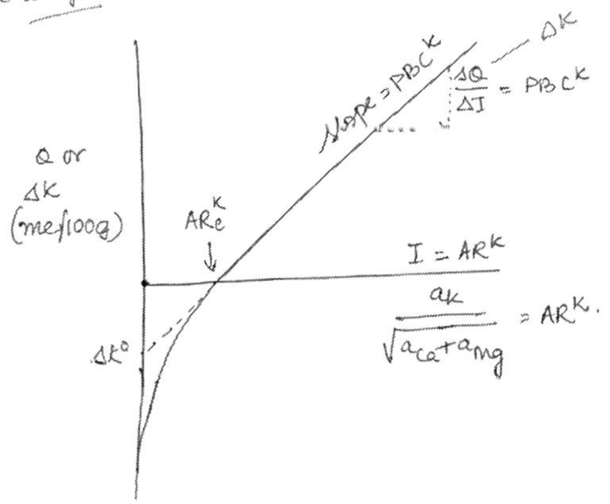

Anion exchange

- At pH Positive charges
- Fe and Al- oxides and amorphous soil colloids mainly
- under suitable conditions — layer silicates.
- At pH < ZPC — surface of mineral — +ve — capacity to attract anions.
- ZPC of Iron oxides ↓ as anion adsorption increases.
- when phosphate adsorbed — +ve charge of oxides — ↓
- with high amounts of P adsorbed — surface — highly negative — accounts for CEC.
- +ve charge at edges of clay minerals
- or broken surfaces of an octahedral sheet. } → significant only at pH values below isoelectric point or ZPC.

- so, broken edged surface → +ve charged double layer at low pH.
- so, double layer becomes increasingly more positive with ↓ soil pH.
- kaolinite — negative charge due to iso. subs. — constant (basal surface)
  - +ve charge on edges.

↓

so amphoteric charac.

↓

so interaction can also occur between these charges — cause self flocculation of kaolinite clays.

Non-specific adsorption

- adsorp. of anions by electrostatic forces on clay minerals and metals.
- outersphere complexation.

a) Negative adsorption

- repulsion of anions from colloidal surfaces — possessing -ve charges

so, anions are expelled from double layer formed by -ve charge surface. → small part of CEC.

↳ cations are attracted.

- only 1-5% of CEC.

↓

15% in saline soils.

CEC = Σ exc. cations − Σ exc. anions.

$$CEC = \frac{\text{layer charge}}{\text{formula wt}} = eq/g$$

- affected by soil pH
  - negative charge density of the colloids
  - valence of anions
  - presence of exc. cations.

↑ density → ↑ adsorption (so, smectite > kaolinite)

↓ pH → ↓ negative charges → ↓ neg. adsorption of anions.

↑ valence charge ⟹ more repelled than ↓ valency.

↑ neg. adsorption → ↑ valence.

neg. adsorption of Cl^- ↓ according to seq. Na > K > Ca > Ba –

presence of Ba on exchange sites results in smallest -ve adsorption whereas Na — ↑ repulsion of Cl^-.

- Wiklander — negative adsorption ↓ with ↑ salt-concn — salts suppresses unequal ion distribution between interface and bulk solution.
- From envn. aspect → -ve adso. harmful process.
- ↓ causes anions to push away from interface into bulk — leaching of anions — imp. nut. sources. → eutrophication — eg. P.

6) Positive adsorption.

- adsorption and concn of anions on +vely charged surfaces/ edges — soil colloids.
- negative adsorp. of cations.
- AEC substantially < CEC.
- dependent on changes in electrolyte levels and soil pH.
- AEC ↑ with ↓ pH.
- AEC — small in smectitic clay
  - ↑ in kaolinitic — but at low pH ~~a~~ — at high pH — repulsion due to ↑ -ve charge.

- Bolt (1976) - lyotropic series

$$SiO_4^{4-} > PO_4^{3-} >> SO_4^{2-} > NO_3^- = Cl^-$$

strongly adsorbed ($SiO_4^{4-} > PO_4^{3-}$); adsorbed in considerably lower concentration ($SO_4^{2-} > NO_3^- = Cl^-$)

Specific adsorption

- Innersphere complexation - Sposito
- oxide, hydrous oxide, amorphous and other variable charge clays.
- concn of anions adsorbed to neutralize +ve charges. —
- caused by displacement of ~~OH or~~ lattice O or OH groups by anions.
- also known as ligand exc, chemisorption, anion penetration

– forces – ionic and especially covalent bonding.

– ~~prevalent in acid soil~~.

– ~~results in strong b~~

eg. Phosphate fixation.

Soil erosion and Conservation

- About 80 mha - India - degraded due to water and wind erosion
- 21 mha - wind erosion
- Out of total degraded land in India, 80% - wet soil erosion
  - ↓ out of which 80% - water erosion.
- Annual loss of soil - 5 $t\ ha^{-1} yr^{-1}$
  - ↓ 80 $t\ ha^{-1} yr^{-1}$
  - national avg - 16 $t\ ha^{-1} yr^{-1}$
- Red soils - mostly affected
  - ↳ due to low intake capacity due to crust
  - ↳ being shallow.
- Shiwaliks - seasonal streams from Shiwaliks - flowing down the submontane areas of different states - Chaos/khads.
- 1.5 mha → every year - clearing of forest land
- 4.5 mha → under shifting cultivation.

Significance of soil erosion

i) Loss of fertile soil - loss of nutrients → 5.4 - 8.4 Mt

ii) Loss of crop productivity

iii) Water pollution - eutrophication

iv) Loss of reservoir capacity - high sediment load in runoff water entering the reservoir → Wular Lake of Kashmir.

v) Flash floods and mudslides.

Causes of soil erosion

i) Deforestation - natural vegetation
  - reduce K.E of raindrop
  - roots bind the soil

ii) Overgrazing - areas of low forage productivity.

iii) Inappropriate cultivation practices - up and down cult.
  - cultivation on sloping land.
  - unsafe disposal of excess runoff

iv) Intensive tillage.

v) Increasing population, pressure → to feed coupled with urbanization

Types of soil erosion

i) Splash erosion

- first stage of erosion
- on bare and exposed land
- raindrops - disperse the aggregates
  - displace the detached part.
- ↑ 0.7 m above ground → 1.5 m horizontally
- form soil crust

ii) Sheet erosion

- removal of soil in uniform layers - sloping lands
- loss of top fertile soil
- generally unnoticed.
- in combination with rill erosion - inter rill erosion.

iii) Rill erosion

- most common
- when excess runoff - gets concentrated due to isolated patches of vegetation or rock pieces - silt laden runoff forms small ephimeral channels
- can be obliterated by tillage before next storm
- discontinuous - no connection with main river system

iv) Gully erosion

- when these channels are eroded to the point - can't be obliterated by tillage
- cross section area of 0.1 m^2 or more. > 30 cm depth.
- permanently dissects the land
- eroded huge amount of salt
- deteoriate water quality

v) Stream Bank erosion:

- runoff over the side of stream bank.
- scouring and undercutting below water surface
- due to ↑ peak flow
- scour erosion more serious than stream bank.
- accelerated by removal of vegetation, overgrazing and tillage near the banks

- ↑ sediment load
- change rivers change their course - leading to flash floods during high intensity rainfall.

vi) Mass movement and landsliding :

- in response to force of gravity
- mass movements - slumping, soil creep, rotational slope, rockfall - rockslide and mudslide.
- Landslide - outward and downward movement of slope forming mat. such as natural rock, soil, artificial fills etc.

Special forms of water erosion

i) Pedestal soil erosion

- when an easily erodible soil. protected by stone or ~~tree~~ rock root
- ~~pedestal~~ isolated pedestals capped by resistant matl.
- form very slowly and found as isolated grazing patches.

ii) Pinnacle

- in highly erodible soils - gully side or bottoms
- capped by resistant mat
- due to physical and chem. charac. of soil eg. due to excessive Na → dispersion.

iii) Tunneling

- Water infiltrates through surface cracks, animal burrows - move down. till it reaches a less permeable layer.
- If fine particles of more porous soil - washed out - sideways erosion - tunneling - joins underground water.
- insidious form of sub-soil surface erosion.

iv) Fertility erosion

- same in magnitude - removal by crops.
- Phosphorus - ~~atten~~ along with colloidal particles where it is attached
- Nitrogen - nitrate and nitrite - solution runoff

Physics of rainfall

i) Quantity of rainfall

- in mm or cm
- eg. 1 cm of deep sheet of rainwater over 1 km^2 represents $10^4 m^3$ of volume of water
- instrument — standard (non-recording gauge) / ~~non~~ recording gauge

ii) Annual distribution of rainfall

- uniform distribution - desirable for vegetation
  ↳ occurs in temperate regions.
- In tropical regions — a single well defined rainy season ↳ unimodal dist.
- Two rainy → bimodal → if dry spell between two storms — allow for crop harvesting and tillage practices, it is agriculturally desirable.

iii) Rainfall intensity

- mmh^{-1}
- speed at rain falls
- storms of high intensity — mostly short duration
- If ↑ duration → ↑ erosion
- recording rain gauge
- slope of curve

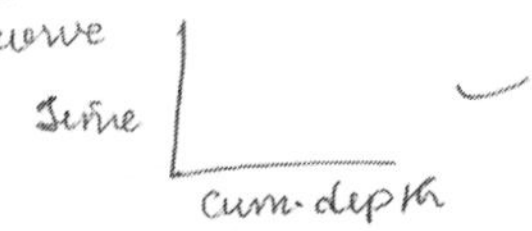

iv) Rain drop size:

- 6 mm
- If >6 mm — detach.
- smaller drops - merge also.

v) Drop size distribution

- Best index - ~~mean~~ median drop diameter (D_{50}) - half of its volume — falls in drops of smaller diameter
  — " " " larger.

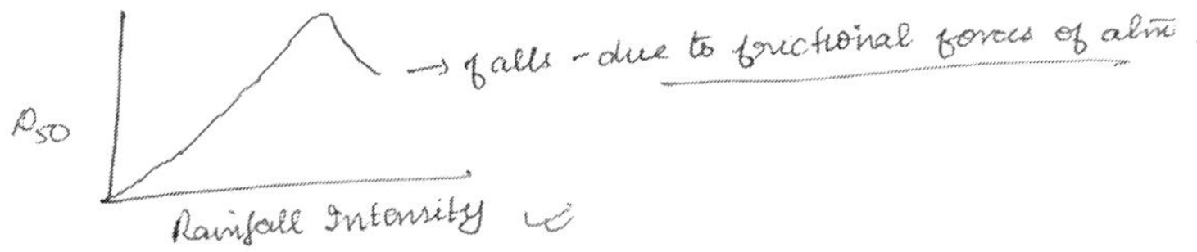

v) Terminal velocity

- body falling freely - under gravity - falls until it reaches a constant speed when frictional resistance of air = gravitational force.
- ↑ size raindrops — ↑ terminal velocity.
- 5m s⁻¹ for 1mm drop   5 ms⁻¹ → 1
- 9m s⁻¹ for 5mm drop   9 m → 5
- most drops - at 10m fall.

vi) Momentum and K.E   K.E = mass × (T.V)²

⇒ KE = (mass) × (T.V)²

Rainfall erosivity

- ability of rainfall to cause erosion.
- function of physical charac. of rainfall
- cumbersome to measure
- so, from indices - Erosivity indices

i) Erosivity Index₃₀ - EI_{30}

- splash, overland flow, rill erosion - affected by compound parameter / index of kinetic energy and maximum 30 minute rainfall intensity (I_{30})

EI_{30} = KE × I_{30} — maximum average rainf. intensity exp. in 30 minute

ii) KE > 25 mmh⁻¹

- KE = 11.87 + 8.73 $\log I_{30}$
- KE > 25 mmh⁻¹ threshold
- But for temperate - 10 mmh⁻¹.

iii) AIm : = amount of rain (A) × maximum Im over 7.5 minute.

For NW India — 15 minute

Soil erodibility

- susceptibility of soil to erosion – detachability
  - transportability

Factors

$T^2 S^2$ WOREP

↳ Texture, structure, water, Rheological, soil profile
Tilth, strength, OM, exc. cations

i) Texture: silt (0.002-0.05 mm) and fine sand (0.05-0.1 mm) are most susceptible
- medium texture – most sus.

ii) Aggregation
- ↑aggregate – water stable
- 0.25 – 5 mm

iii) Tilth
- rough cloddy surface – resistant
- fine tilth – suscep.

iv) Strength
- resistance towards shearing forces
- ↓ with ↑ MC

v) Water
- reduces its cohesiveness

vi) OM

vii) Rheological: prop of soil water system in moist to semi fluid state – Initiation of tunnel erosion in cracking clay.

viii) exc. cation

ix) Profile — sand over clay, shallow close to bedrock] erosion

6

~~DCESE~~

Erodibility Indices

- tedious to measure soil erodibility | DCESE |

i) Dispersion ratio = $\frac{\text{silt + clay in undispersed}}{\text{disperse}}$

↑ → ↑ soil ero.

ii) Clay ratio = $\frac{\text{sand + silt}}{\text{clay}}$

iii) Erosion ratio = $\frac{\text{dispersion ratio}}{\frac{\text{clay}}{\text{Moisture equivalent}}}$

iv) Surface aggregation ratio = $\frac{\text{surface area of part} \geq 0.05\,mm}{\text{aggregated silt + clay}}$

(silt + clay in dis − undis)

- more reliable index due to its imp on soil agg.

v) Erosion Index = inverse of ~~rain~~ no. of raindrops - to break down completely an aggregate

Kukal et al (2008) - EI_{SRT} — kinetic energy to completely disperse using single rain drop technique.

Factors affecting soil erosion | C.SVT |

i) climate

ii) soil

iii) Vegetation :

IRPABT

~~IRBA~~

i) Interception effect

ii) decreasing surface runoff

iii) restrict physical movement of soil PIRBAT

iv) improve soil aggregation

v) enhance biological activity

vi) Transpiration - H_2O deficit in roots

iv) Topography

↑ → ↑ slope

- Concave slope with lower slope at foothill - less erosive.

Processes and mechanics of soil erosion

- Two phase
- Detachment
  - rain splash
  - weathering
  - tillage practices
  - trampling of soil by people and livestock
  - running water
- Transportation
  - → act aerially – remove uniform thickness.
    - overland flow
  - → concentrate in a channels.
    - gullies
  - → under the gravity.
    - soil flows and slides.
- 2 categores
  - detachment limited
  - transport limited

Runoff

- Runoff is portion of ppt – that joins the rivers or oceans as surface or subsurface flow.
- water starts moving from depression - storage – overland flow ↳ surface
- if water percolates without joining H_2O table – sub surf.

Factors

TIDDADCC

↳ Type of ppt
↳ Intensity
↳ duration
↳ distribution – dist. coefficient = $\frac{\text{max}^m\ \text{rain at a point}}{\text{mean rainfall on entire catchment}}$
↳ Antecedant soil moistu
↳ climate
↳ ~~C~~atchment area — fan shaped area > more runoff – lower time of concn (outlet from remotest) —
↳ ~~Dural~~ Direction of prevailing storm

- to drainage texture (no. of 1st order streams/area)
  density (length of all stream/area)

Measurement

(i) small plots - reservoirs at down slope end of the plot
  - measure on volume basis.

(ii) streams :- stream stage : elevation of water surface in ref. to a standard datum

gauges → staff - graduated staff
→ wire gauge - wt - lowered by rope/wire.

Assessment of soil erosion

i) Soil Loss Tolerance

- soil conservation society -
  - max^m rate of soil loss - tolerated - without any long term reduction in the productive capacity of soil.

ii) Soil erosion assessment surveys.

- using aerial photo and satellite imageries. → more cheaper, repetitive exposures.

i) static surveys - at an area.

ii) sequential - two or more dates

iii) dynamics - factors

iii) Universal soil loss equation

$A = R \times K \times L \times S \times C \times P$ → cm h^{-1}

R → $\frac{EI_{30}}{100}$ = MJ ha^{-1} mm^{-1}

A → amt in soil loss (t ha^{-1} yr^{-1})

Basic Principles of soil Conservation

(i) Covering surface
(ii) ↑ aggregate stability
(iii) ↑ infiltration
(iv) ↑ surface roughness
(v) Reducing runoff
(vi) safe disposal of excessive runoff.

CAISRD

SAICRD

Agronomic measures — role of veg. — protection to soil.
— both detachment and transport phase

Mechanical — manipulate surface topography
— only transport phase
— more expensive.

Agronomic measures

CSC VSF GMO CASS

↳ Cover crops
↳ strip cropping
↳ selection of crop sp. and crop rotation
↳ vegetative barrier
↳ Forest and plantation management
↳ Grazing land manag.
↳ Mulching
↳ OM
↳ Conservation tillage
↳ A — Agroforestry
— soil stabilizers/conditioners
— Shifting cultivation.

- Cover crops
- close growing crops
- quick to establish
- early canopy cover

Strip croppinig
- 3-8.5°

Crop rotation
- legumes and grasses

Vegetative barrier
- buffer strip cropp
- 3-4 m wide - 10-20 m interval - form bench type terraces
- vetiver zizanoids

Shifting cult
- fallow period > 7 years

Mulching
- OM
- Conservation tillage — no tillage, strip, minimal, mulch

- Agroforestry
- Grazing
- 30-40% exploitation ×
- 70% ground cover
- s

Engineering Practices (CPCTW)

- Temporary or permanent

- i) Contouring : ploughing, planting, cult – along contours
  - reduce 50% erosion – up and down
  - length 30 m – 5.5°
    20 m – 8.5°.
- ii) soil pitting / range pitting – (50 cm × 50 cm × 7.5 cm) – 40 cm apart
- iii) Contour bunds – 1.5-2 m wide – waterstorage
  - 10-20 m interval – permanent buffer strip.
- iv) Terracing — broad channels
  - reduces length of hillside slope
  - diversion
  - retention → permeable $< 4.5°$
  - Bench – shelves and risers (plant) → upto 30°.
- v) Waterways : safe disposal.

Gully control

- i) Veg.
- ii) Mech
  - Loose rock dam
  - Single fench brushwood dam
  - Double " " ".
  - Brick weirs.

Landslides

- Falls (fast, abrupt)
- Creep (slow
- Debris flow
- Debris avalanche (rapid)
- Mudflow (atleast 50% sand silt and clay part)

Factors

- Gravity
- Geological – permeable over imp.
- Heavy rainfall
- Earthq
- Forest fires
- Inapp tillage sys.
- Cutting and deep excavation
- developmental act.
- Change in slope use pattern.

- IWDP – Integrated Water Development Progr – 2008.

Rain Water Harvesting

↳ Insitu – enhance infiltration – within the field where crops grown.

↳ Ex-situ – ponds and reservoirs.

↳ Roof top Rain H_2O.

Soil erosion by wind

- detachment and transportation by wind.
- 13.5 Mha.

Causes

- wind regime (strong)
- low atm. humidity
- high solar radiation
- single grain structure
- removal of vegetal cover
- Extension of agri. to marginal areas.

Mechanism

- Detachment — lifting and abrasive action.
- soil movement — due to turbulence and velocity.

3 forces are involved.

I) Lift — caused by Bernoulli or Venturi effect — air moving ↑ vel. has low pressure ↓ causes bodies to move in direction of pressure differential.

II) Drag — particles stay in motion once init

III) Ballistic impact → collision of part among themselves.

- Transportation
  - → Surface creep — rolling — coarse grains along surface — >0.5 mm.
  - → Saltation: — series of jumps — ~~<1mm~~ 50-70%.
  - → Suspension — fine part <0.2.

- Deposition.

Management

- Inter tilled crops such as corn – sown across the slope
- close growing crops . . . legumes, grass – max eff.
- strips of upright growing crop – across direction of prev. wind.
- strip cropping
- Permanent grass stripes.
- Rough tillage.
- Stubble mulch tillage.
- drought resistant crop.

Windbreak and Shelterbelt — strictly living windbreaks.

- any type of barrier for protection from winds – commonly ass. with mech. or veg – barriers
- 50 feet ht – protect an area approx of one-quarter mile
- density of belt → equivalent porosity of 40-50%.
- align shelt. in parallel rows at ⊥ angle to it
- Belt length min 12 times belt ht. – provided belt is ⊥ angle to wind.
- plant tolerant to wind.